CIRCULAR WALKS
IN THE DYFI VALLEY

Circular Walks
in the Dyfi Valley

Dorothy Hamilton

ISBN: 0-86381-688-6

Cover design: Alan Jones

First published in 2001 by
Gwasg Carreg Gwalch, 12 Iard yr Orsaf, Llanrwst, Wales LL26 0EH
℡ 01492 642031   ▤ 01492 641502
✆ books@carreg-gwalch.co.uk   Internet: www.carreg-gwalch.co.uk

Contents

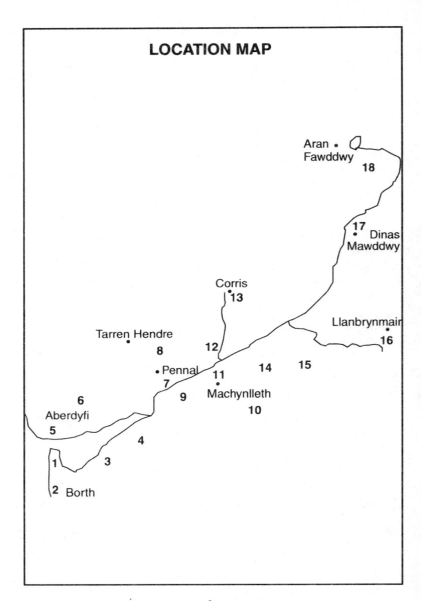

LOCATION MAP

Aran •
Fawddwy   **18**

17
• Dinas
Mawddwy

Corris
•**13**

Llanbrynmair
•**16**

Tarren Hendre
•
8   **12**

7 • Pennal   **11**
•   **14**   **15**
9   Machynlleth
6   **10**
Aberdyfi
5   **4**

1
       3
2 Borth

Introduction

Walks in this guide range from easy, level walks, taking a couple of hours, to all day mountain routes. The walks selected highlight the varied, beautiful landscape and historical interest of the Dyfi Valley. Several walks visit nature reserves and other places of interest.

All the walks have sketch maps and easy to follow directions. The starting points are at, or near, a car park or parking place. Directions are given to reach the start by car and, where possible, by public transport. Bus and train timetables are available from Tourist Information Centres.

The walks are graded according to length and terrain. Easy routes have low mileage and ascents are gentle or short. Moderate walks have longer uphill sections. The walks classed as strenuous reach the mountain tops. The average time taken to complete each walk is given, but extra time may be needed for food breaks, bird watching, photography etc. Although adequate route descriptions are given to follow the walks without referring to other maps, it is advisable to carry the relevant maps on mountain routes. The Ordnance Survey 1:25 000 Outdoor Leisure Sheet 23 covers the guide's high level walks on the Tarren and Aran mountains, as well as most of the other walks. Points of Interest are included for each walk, and these give background information relating to the landscape and historical interest of the area. Facilities list alternative parking, public toilets, pubs, cafes and places to visit.

The majority of walks do not pass refreshment places, therefore, on the longer routes it is advisable to carry some food and drink for snacks along the way. All the routes require sturdy footwear and boots are advisable on the mountains. Take care – choose good weather for the high level walks and be prepared by carrying waterproofs and extra clothing.

Background

Traditionally the boundary between north and south Wales, the beautiful Dyfi valley is now the meeting place of the counties of Gwynedd, Powys and Dyfed. The source of its river, Afon Dyfi, is Creiglyn Dyfi, a lonely lake nestling below the Aran mountains in the south-eastern corner of the Snowdonia National Park.

On its journey to the sea, Afon Dyfi is joined by many tributary rivers and streams, and flows through a great variety of scenery. Starting its journey as Llaethnant, a milky stream that cascades rapidly down the mountainside, the river is fed by other tumbling streams near the hamlet of Llanymawddwy. At first closed in by steep hills, the valley opens out at Dinas Mawddwy, and Afon Dyfi reaches its confluence with Afon Cleifion at Mallwyd. After twisting its way through a deep chasm, the river flows through peaceful countryside, bordered to the west by the extensive coniferous plantations of the Dyfi Forest, and to the east by the wind turbine lined plateau of Mynydd y Cemaes. At Glantwymyn (Cemaes Road), Afon Twymyn and the Cambrian Railway join the Dyfi valley and a few miles farther on Afon Dulas, which flows through the old slate mining village of Corris, adds its waters to the river.

A stone bridge, built in 1805, crosses Afon Dyfi at Machynlleth, the valley's chief town. South of here the river becomes tidal, and at Derwenlas there was once a busy port. Near Glandyfi is the remains of a motte and bailey castle on a knoll overlooking the river, and a nature reserve consisting of woodlands, meadows and marshlands. Farther west are the tidal sands of Traeth Maelgwn, Cors Fochno bog and Ynys-las dunes. In contrast, on the north bank of Afon Dyfi, steep wooded hills border the winding road and railway line that run beside the river. In a lovely situation, at the mouth of Afon Dyfi, is the pretty village of Aberdyfi.

Like aber Mawddach to the north, the Dyfi estuary is the product of glacial deepening and rising sea level. Before the last Ice Age, plains extended into what is now Cardigan Bay. The remains of a forest may be seen on the beach near Ynys-las at low tide. The rock strata of the valley is mainly Silurian deposits, with rocks from the Ordovician era in the area that is now Snowdonia. The Aran mountains, along with Snowdonia's other mountains, are formed from igneous rocks, from which the sedimentary rocks have worn away.

The earliest evidence of man in Wales comes from Pontnewydd near Denbigh, where stone artefacts have been found dating to about 225,000 BC. They belonged to Neanderthal (Old Stone Age) man, who hunted over great distances. The following Ice Ages had periods of mild climate in-between. Nevertheless, the Neanderthals died out about 26,000 BC. At the end of the last Ice Age pine, birch and hazel forests grew and Mesolithic people (Middle Stone Age) left evidence of their presence in Powys. At this time, areas that are now sea would have been marshland with wildfowl. Agriculture arrived about 4,000 BC in the Neolithic (New Stone Age) era when crops such as barley, and domestic animals, came into Britain from the eastern Mediterranean. These people led a more settled life and left behind great stone tombs. In the early Bronze Age people moved into the uplands and many monuments from their presence survive. Stone circles, standing stones and round cairns belong to this period and remains are seen on several walks.

Celtic peoples came to Wales from Central Europe about 600 BC, the start of the Iron Age. Although they lived in farmsteads and centred their lives around agriculture, they built defensive forts on the tops of hills (see Walk 15). The Romans invaded Britain in AD 43 and by AD 78 they had control of Wales. They built a fort near Afon Dyfi at Pennal. The Roman road, Sarn Helen, passed through the valley on its way from *Canovium*, near Conwy, to *Moridunum* at Caerfyrddin (Carmarthen).

After the Roman withdrawal, Wales was divided into small kingdoms. A number of Celtic missionaries, mainly from Ireland and Brittany, came to the west coast of Britain and set up monasteries, churches and Celtic crosses. Several churches in the Dyfi valley were founded at this time.

For short periods Wales was one kingdom. In the 9th century, Rhodri Mawr (the Great) was the first man to unite Wales politically, partly by his marrying Angharad, heiress of Ceredigion. His grandson Hywel Dda (the Good) also briefly united north and south Wales by marriage. He made a pilgrimage to Rome in 928. When he died, Wales was again divided into small princedoms.

After 1066 the Normans slowly penetrated Wales by building motte and bailey castles. Gilbert de Clare built such a castle in 1110 near Aberystwyth. Henry I's death in 1142 left a disputed succession and Wales regained confidence. Rhys ap Gruffudd (Lord Rhys) built an earthwork castle overlooking Afon Dyfi in 1156 at a time when Owain Gwynedd was threatening Ceredigion. It proved unnecessary but was taken two years later by Roger de Clare then retaken in the same year by Rhys. Henry II's disastrous campaign in the Berwyn mountains in 1165 (he was defeated by the bog and the rain) gave Wales a revival. Rhys held the first gathering of the bards at Aberteifi (Cardigan) in 1177 and he also endowed a Cistercian monastery at Strata Florida.

Llywelyn ap Iorwerth, the grandson of Owain Gwynedd, became the most powerful of the medieval princes. After taking castles in south Wales, his military achievements were rewarded with the title Lord of Snowdon. His grandson Llywelyn ap Gruffudd (the Last) was also powerful enough to be recognised Prince of Wales by Henry III. However conflict with the next English king, Edward I, resulted in war and, eventually, Llywelyn was killed near Builth Wales. This brought an end to Welsh independence and Llywelyn's principality was divided into English type shires. Merionethshire (Meirionnydd) and Cardiganshire (Ceredigion) were two such counties. East and south Wales were in the hands of the Marcher lords. Aberystwyth castle is one of the many castles Edward I built to consolidate his victory.

In 1400, Owain Glyndŵr led an uprising against English rule

which was to last several years. Amongst the castles he captured were Aberystwyth and Harlech. He held parliament in Machynlleth in 1404 and may have been crowned there. With French support the following year, he invaded England, but eventually retreated followed by Henry IV's troops, who found the fords impassable and returned to England. From Pennal, in 1406, Owain Glyndŵr wrote to the French king, Charles VI, setting out his manifesto. He wanted two universities in Wales. Charles returned greetings, but did not send the army that Owain needed. At this point in time, Owain still controlled most of Wales, but after a long siege, Aberystwyth castle fell in 1408 and Harlech a year later. How Owain ended his days is a mystery.

This is sheep country and until the Industrial Revolution the woollen industry was important in the Dyfi valley and surrounding hills. Afon Dyfi is well known for its salmon, and poaching has undoubtedly played a large part in the history of the river. Dense oak woods in the valley were felled for ship building and timber products were exported from the quays at Derwen-las. Nowadays, sheep farming remains important, but coniferous plantations replace many of the oak woods. The coming of the railway in the mid 19th century brought tourists to Machynlleth and Cardigan Bay. Today, tourism is a major industry as more people discover this fascinating, unspoilt, beautiful valley in the heart of Wales.

Welsh Place Names

The following words are sometimes used in place names in the Dyfi valley.

Aber – estuary, river mouth
Afon – river
Bach/Fach – small
Banc – bank, hill
Bedd – grave
Blaen – head (of valley)
Bryn – hill
Bwlch – pass
Bychan – little
Cae – field
Caer/Gaer – fort
Cam – step, crooked
Canol – middle, centre
Capel – chapel
Carreg – stone
Castell – castle
Cau – deep hollow
Cefn – ridge
Celli/Gelli – grove
Ceunant – ravine
Coch – red
Coed – woodland, trees
Cors/Gors – bog, marsh
Craig – rock
Croes – cross
Cwm – valley
Cwrt – court
Derwen – oak tree
Dinas – fort
Dôl/Ddôl – meadow

Drum – ridge
Drws – door
Du/Ddu – black
Dŵr – water
Dyffryn – valley, dale
Eglwys – church
Enw(au) – name(s)
Erw – acre
Esgair – hill spur
Ffordd – road
Ffos – ditch
Ffridd – mountain pasture
Ffynnon – spring, well
Gallt/Allt – hillside, slope
Garn – cairn
Glan – riverbank
Glas – blue
Grug – heather
Gwastad – plain, level ground
Gwaun/Waun – moor
Gwyn – white
Hafod/Hafoty – summer dwelling
Hen – old
Hendre – winter dwelling
Heol – road
Hir – long
Isaf – lower
Lôn – lane
Llan – church
Llech – slate
Llethr – slope
Llidiart – gate
Llwybr – path
Llwyd – grey
Llyn – lake

Llys – court, palace
Maen – stone
Maethlon – nourishing
Mawr/Fawr – big, great, large
Melin/Felin – mill
Moel/Foel – bare hill, mountain top
Morfa – marsh
Mynydd/Fynydd – mountain
Mur – wall
Nant – stream
Neuadd – hall
Newydd – new
Ogof – cave
Pandy – fulling-mill
Pant – hollow, valley
Parc – park, field
Pen – head, top
Pentre – village
Pistyll – spout, cataract
Plas – mansion
Pont – bridge
Porth – port
Pwll – pool
Rhiw – hill
Rhos – moorland, heath
Rhyd – ford
Sarn – causeway, road
Sych – dry
Tan – under
Tarren – hill, knoll
Tir – land
Tomen – mound
Traeth – beach
Tre/Tref – town
Trwyn – promontory

Twll – hole
Tŷ – house
Tyddyn – small-holding, small farm
Uchaf – upper
Uwch – above, higher
Y/Yr – the
Ynys – island
Ysgol – school
Ysgubor – barn
Ystrad – valley floor

Information Centres

Borth Tourist Information Centre	01970 871174
Aberdyfi Tourist Information Centre	01654 767321
Machynlleth Tourist Information Centre	01654 702401
Corris Tourist Information Centre	01654 761244
Ynys-las Centre	01970 871640
Ynys-hir Nature Reserve	01654 781265
Centre for Alternative Technology	01654 702400

Country Code

1. Guard against any risk of fire.
2. Keep to the public rights of way when crossing farmland.
3. Avoid causing any damage to walls, fences and hedges.
4. Leave farm gates as you find them.
5. Keep dogs under control in the presence of livestock.
6. Leave machinery, farm animals and crops alone.
7. Take care not to pollute water.
8. Carry your litter home with you.
9. Protect all wildlife, plants and trees.
10. Avoid making any unnecessary noise.
11. Drive carefully on country roads.
12. Enjoy and respect the countryside.

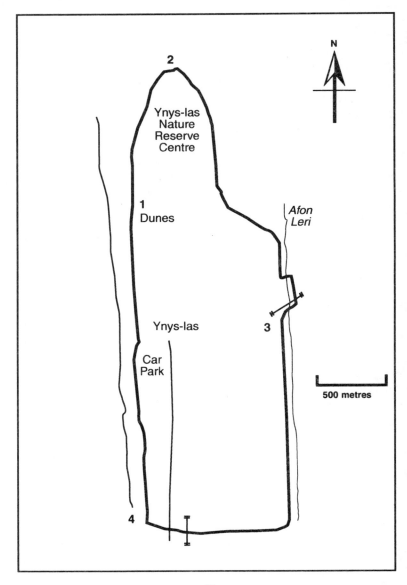

N

2

Ynys-las
Nature
Reserve
Centre

1
Dunes

*Afon
Leri*

Ynys-las

3

Car
Park

500 metres

4

Ynys-las – Pont Aber Leri – Afon Leri – Ynys-las

OS Maps:	1:50 000 Landranger Sheet 135;
	1:25 000 Outdoor Leisure Sheet 23.
Start:	Car park at Ynys-las, above the beach. This is at the point where the B4353 turns away from the coast. G.R. 606925.
Access:	Ynys-las is north of Borth on the B4352. Buses from Aberystwyth to Ynys-las.
Parking:	Car park at Ynys-las.
Grade:	Easy – beach, tracks and riverside paths. Level.
Time:	3-3½ hours.

Points of Interest:

1. Ynys-las dunes form part of the Dyfi National Nature Reserve. The dunes provide a habitat for many plants and insects. Sea spurge, lady's bedstraw, rest harrow, ragwort, bird's foot trefoil and violets are some of the plants that may be found. Orchids grow in the damp hollows. Lizards, rabbits, voles, stoats and polecats are present. The dunes also provide a habitat for butterflies, moths, beetles and spiders, especially the wolf spider.

2. Many wading birds and wildfowl visit the estuary to feed. Waders include ringed plover, dunlin, redshank, curlew and oystercatcher. Winter is the best time to see wildfowl, when widgeon, pintail and Greenland white-fronted geese may be present. The beach to the east is Traeth Maelgwn. It is said that Maelgwn Gwynedd met his rivals (from Deheubarth and

Powys) on this beach to settle their dispute over rulership. They sat in chairs on the beach and waited for the tide. The winner was the last to remain in his chair. Because Maelgwn's chair was built with waxed feathers, it floated whilst the others submerged, and he became king. The 'event' is celebrated as part of Borth Carnival.

3. Snipe, teal, water rail and reed bunting may be seen from the embankment. On the opposite side of Afon Leri is the Cors Fochno National Nature Reserve, one of the largest peat bogs in lowland Britain. Many uncommon moths are found there, also otters. Birds of prey, including harriers, may be seen flying overhead.

4. At one time the coastline was several miles farther west. At low tide, tree stumps are exposed on the beach. These are the remains of a forest that was submerged at the end of the last Ice Age.

Walk Directions: (–) denotes Point of Interest

1. From the car park walk out to the beach and bear right. Pass the Ynys-las dunes (1) and continue north in the direction of Aberdyfi.

2. Follow the high water mark around the estuary (2), passing (in the nesting season) a roped off section on your left. A path through the dunes leads to the Ynys-las Nature Reserve Centre.

3. Continue your walk along the beach. Pass along the edge of the salt marsh and, shortly before meeting Afon Leri, turn right on a track. Pass the boatyard and emerge on the B4353. Turn left to cross a bridge over Afon Leri.

4. In a few metres go through a small gate on the right. Walk beside the river to a level crossing. Exercise great care at this point – listen to check that no trains are coming before you cross. Cross the railway line and then the railway bridge over Afon Leri. Bear left onto an embankment and cross a stile.

5. Continue ahead through the Aberleri – Dyfi nature reserve (3). In 1.7 km, about 50 metres before reaching some gates on the embankment, turn right on a track. Pass a bird hide (usually open) and go over a level crossing to the B4353.

6. Cross the road to the beach (4) and bear right to return to the start at the car park.

Facilities:

Parking, Information and public toilets at Ynys-las nature reserve centre (open March – September). Ice cream van on the beach in the summer. Camp sites nearby.

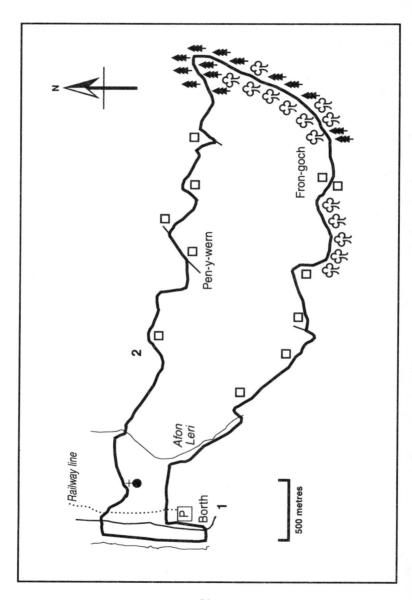

Railway line

Borth

P

1

500 metres

Afon Leri

2

Pen-y-wern

Fron-goch

N

Borth – Pen-y-wern – Fron-goch – Afon Leri – Borth

OS Maps:	1:50 000 Landranger Sheet 135;
	1:25 000 Explorer Sheet 213.
Start:	Borth sea front at the junction of the B4353 and B4572. G.R. 608890.
Access:	Borth is north of Aberystwyth, 2½ miles (3.8 km) off the A487. Buses from Aberystwyth. Trains from Machynlleth and Aberystwyth.
Parking:	Near roadside, Borth sea front.
Grade:	Moderate – field, woodland and riverside paths, tracks and lanes.
Time:	About 4 hours.

Points of Interest:

1. The attractive seaside resort of Borth was a small fishing village, until the arrival of the railway in 1863 brought visitors to the long sandy beach. Tree stumps of a submerged forest are uncovered on the shore at low tide. About halfway between Borth and Aberystwyth, the causeway called Sarn Cynfelyn stretches out for several miles into Cardigan Bay. According to legend, it is the remains of the lost lands of Cantre'r Gwaelod. Long ago, where Cardigan Bay is now, there was a fertile plain which had sixteen cities. A system of dykes and sluices gave protection from the sea. In the 6th century, during the reign of Gwyddno Garanhir, the drunkard Seithennyn failed to carry out his job of closing the sluices. Cantre'r Gwaelod and all its peoples were drowned for ever. Geological investigations have revealed that Cardigan Bay was once a plain, which was gradually encroached upon by the sea. This, however, probably took place at the end of the last Ice Age.

2. The National Nature Reserve of Cors Fochno (Borth bog) is one of the best preserved lowland peat bogs in Britain. It was once much larger than it is now. Between 1820 and 1960, 1200 hectares of tidal marsh and bog were reclaimed and converted into farmland. Until the early 20th century, peat was cut from the edge of the bog and used as fuel by local people. According to legend, the bog was inhabited by a seven foot tall witch called Yr Hen Wrach. She got into people's houses and caused illness. Since Cors Fochno became a nature reserve, measures have been taken to help the bog retain its rainfall. This involves damming old ditches and channels. The most important of the bog plants are the mosses and fourteen species occur in the reserve. Cotton grass, sundew and bog asphodel are some of the other plants that grow here. Otters are present. Birds include teal, curlew, reed bunting and skylark. Several uncommon species of moths have been found. A public footpath runs along the south edge of the reserve but to visit other parts, a permit is necessary. This can be obtained from the Ynys-las nature reserve centre.

Walk Directions: (–) denotes Point of Interest

1. At the junction of roads in Borth (1), if the tide is out, walk onto the beach and bear right. Alternatively, follow the B4353 in the direction of Ynys-las. If following the beach, leave it in approximately 900 metres, at the seventh long breakwater, and walk up the shingle to the road. At this point, there are no buildings on the seaward side of the road.

2. Take a narrow lane just before reaching the Golf Hotel. (There is a sign for the church.) Pass a chapel and bear right. Cross the railway line with care and walk in the direction of the church.

3. Bear left to pass the church gates on your right. Go through a kissing gate (next to a broad gate) and walk below a small hill. Cross a stile and follow a fence on the left. After crossing another stile go up to the embankment above Afon Leri.

4. Bear right and in approximately 50 metres cross a footbridge over the river. Turn left and in a few metres leave the embankment to cross a stile that is below on your right. In a few paces cross a footbridge over a channel. Follow the right boundary of the field for about 100 metres then cross the field diagonally left to the far corner.

5. Cross a stile next to a gate and follow a track past a building. On reaching a lane, bear left and go through a gate. As you walk uphill, you will have good views on your left of Cors Fochno (2). Pass a house and other buildings. Where the track bends to the left, leave it to go through the gate ahead.

6. Walk uphill and follow a fence on the left. Cross a stile and continue along the left boundary of the field. Go uphill to the next stile. From here there are fine views of the Dyfi estuary. In a few paces bear left to cross a stream. Walk beside a line of trees and bushes to the next stile. Continue beside a left-hand fence to a stile and lane.

7. Bear left past Pen-y-wern and in approximately 300 metres turn right on a track towards a bungalow. Go through the gate ahead and walk up the field to find a stile near the top left-hand corner.

8. Follow an old track between trees and go through a gate. Continue along the edge of the field and go through the next gate. Bear slightly left to a stile below the farm. Go ahead to a stile near a gate.

9. Follow the right-hand boundary of the field around two sides. Cross a stile and walk along the right side of this field to a stile at a corner. Pass buildings on the left and follow the hedge to another stile and lane.

10. Turn left and in just over 100 metres, cross a stile on the right. Walk ahead, uphill, along the right boundaries of fields. Descend to the edge of a wood and cross a stile. Follow the path that slants to the left, downhill, through coniferous trees.

11. On reaching a track at a bend, continue ahead, downhill. Emerge on a wider track, where there is a barrier on the left. Turn right and ignore another track on the left. Continue through mixed woods and in approximately another 300 metres, ignore a path on the right.

12. Stay on the main track and pass through an area where there is some heather and gorse. Ignore paths on the right and, 100 metres after passing a track (also on the right) and just before the track you are walking on goes downhill, bear right on a clear path. It passes above the main track.

13. In a few metres, the path starts to descend. On reaching a fork, take the right-hand path. Rejoin the main track and continue ahead to a gate and field.

14. Cross the field by going slightly uphill to join a track that passes between trees and gorse. Continue ahead and pass the ruined farmhouse called Fron-goch on your right. Walk uphill to the top left-hand boundary of the field and pass through a gate in the corner into the next field.

15. Bear left into another field. Cross, descending slightly, towards the far corner. Pass a fence on the right and trees on the left to find a stile near a bridle gate. Walk ahead and bear right to pass behind a farmhouse. Cross a stile and leave the next

field by going through a gate on the left.

16. Turn right on the track to emerge on a lane. Turn left and, after passing a house on the right, reach a lane junction. Bear left around a bend and, in approximately 30 metres, turn right on a narrow lane.

17. Pass a farm on the right and turn left at a junction. At the end of the lane bear left into some trees. Cross a footbridge over Afon Leri and immediately turn right on a footpath. Pass a caravan site on the left. Go through a kissing gate and walk ahead with the river on your right.

18. Pass through another kissing gate to have a track parallel to the path. On reaching the lane to the Animalarium, bear left to follow it towards Borth. Cross the railway at the level crossing and reach the B4353 in Borth. Turn left to return to the start of the walk.

Facilities:

Refreshments in Borth. Public toilets near the start of the walk. Animalarium. Several campsites in the area.

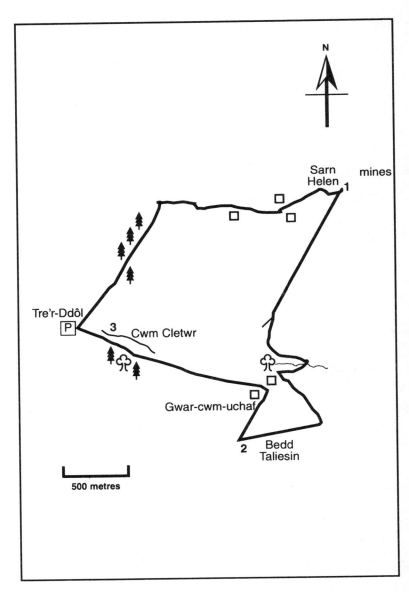

N

Sarn
Helen
1

mines

Tre'r-Ddôl
P

3 Cwm Cletwr

Gwar-cwm-uchaf

2 Bedd
Taliesin

500 metres

Tre'r-ddôl – Sarn Helen – Bedd Taliesin – Tre'r-ddôl

OS Maps:	1:50 000 Landranger Sheet 135; 1:25 000 Outdoor Leisure Sheet 23
Start:	The Wildfowler Inn, Tre'r-ddôl. G.R. 659923.
Access:	Tre'r-ddôl is off the A487, 8½ miles (13.5 km) south of Machynlleth. Buses from Machynlleth and Aberystwyth pass through Tre'r-ddôl.
Parking:	Near the Wildfowler pub.
Grade:	Moderate – woodland and field paths, tracks and lanes.
Time:	3-3½ hours.

Points of Interest:

1. Sarn Helen is a Roman Road linking the forts between Caerhun, near Conwy, and *Moridunum* at Caerfyrddin (Carmarthen). Sarn means road and, according to tradition, it was named after the wife of the Roman Emperor, Macsen Wledig (Magnus Maximus). According to the story in *Y Mabinogion*, the Emperor dreamt of a lady in a far off land. When he woke up he remembered his dream and sent messengers around the world to look for her. After searching for a long time, they found Elen at Aber Saint, near Caernarfon. The emperor came to Wales and married Elen and, at her request, built a road linking south and north Wales – hence Sarn Helen. The remains of the Bryndyfi lead mines are located about 200 metres north-east of the lane junction. At the end of the 19th century, about one hundred men worked in the mines,

but they closed after about two years as only a small amount of lead ore was found.

2. Bedd Taliesin is a Bronze Age cairn dating from about 2,000 BC. In the centre there is a two metre long grave where, according to rumour, a skull was once found. The cairn is reputed to contain the bones of Taliesin, the 6th century Welsh poet, greatest of all bards. Legend has it that he was found as a baby in a coracle caught on a fishing weir near Borth by Elffin, the son of Gwyddno Garanhir. When Taliesin grew up he rescued Elffin from a dungeon in Deganwy castle.

3. Cwm Cletwr is a Site of Special Scientific Interest. The 52 acre nature reserve consists of sessile oak and ash woodlands, with a wide variety of mosses and lichens. Flowers include yellow archangel, dog's mercury and woodruff. Look out for dippers and woodpeckers.

Walk Directions: (–) denotes Point of Interest

1. Facing the Wildfowler Inn, turn right and follow the road to the A487. Turn right and, in approximately 100 metres (just before a lay-by) bear right to follow a path into woodland.

2. When the path forks, bear left and walk uphill to meet a forest track. Turn left and follow it to a lane. Bear right along this quiet lane, past farms, to reach a junction with another lane, the Roman Road, Sarn Helen (1).

3. Turn right and, at the next junction, ignore a lane on the right. Descend through trees to a bridge across Afon Cletwr. Walk uphill on the lane and, before reaching the farm buildings of Gwar-cwm-uchaf, turn left on a clear track.

4. The track passes between fields and follows a stream on the left. In about 600 metres it joins another track. From here, there are fine views of the Dyfi estuary.

5. Turn right along the firm track. Go through a gate across it and, a few metres before reaching a lane, you will see Bedd Taliesin (2) on your left.

6. Walk ahead to join the lane and turn right. Go through a gate and follow the lane as far as Gwar-cwm-uchaf.

7. After passing the house, and before reaching other buildings, bear left to go through a gate. Pass the house on your left and follow a track. Go through a gate and cross a stream. Continue beside a left-hand fence and pass through a small patch of woodland.

8. Go through a small gate to pass above a stream. Follow a fence on the right but, when it bears right, walk ahead across the field.

9. Join a track and go through a gate across it. Continue on the track, which gives fine views of the surrounding countryside and Dyfi estuary. Enter a wood and descend on a clear path that bends right and left. On reaching a gate, ignore the steep descending path beside it.

10. Go through the gate and continue on a path through coniferous trees. Pass through more gates and join another path above Afon Cletwr. Turn right if you wish to explore Cwm Cletwr Nature Reserve (3).

11. Return along the path to have the river on your right. Descend to a track and follow it to the road in Tre'r-ddôl. Turn right and cross the bridge to return to the start of the walk and the Wildfowler Inn.

Facilities:

Refreshments at the Wildfowler Inn. Yr Hen Gapel Museum in Tre'r-ddôl.

Walk 4   *6 miles (9.5 kilometres)*

Furnace – Ynys-hir – Domen Las – Furnace

OS Maps:	1:50 000 Landranger Sheet 135; 1:25 000 Outdoor Leisure Sheet 23.
Start:	Dyfi Furnace (Cadw monument) in the village of Furnace. G.R. 685952.
Access:	Furnace is on the A487, 7 miles (11 km) south-west of Machynlleth. Buses from Aberystwyth and Machynlleth.
Parking:	Car park along surfaced track opposite the Dyfi Furnace.
Grade:	Easy/Moderate – Paths, tracks and lane. Most of the walk is through a nature reserve – dogs not allowed – for which there is a charge (unless you are a RSPB member).
Time:	3½-4 hours.

Points of Interest:

1. The name Furnace comes from the impressive monument next to the waterfall on Afon Einion. The blast furnace was built as part of an ironworks in about 1755 by Jonathan Kendall from Staffordshire. Iron ore was shipped from Cumberland to a nearby port on Afon Dyfi. Charcoal produced from local deciduous woods provided fuel for the furnace. A channel was built to carry water from Afon Einion to the water-wheel that powered the bellows. The blast provided the high temperatures necessary to smelt iron. Dyfi Furnace was in use for about fifty years. After being abandoned the building was taken over as a sawmill. The water-wheel dates from that period of time.

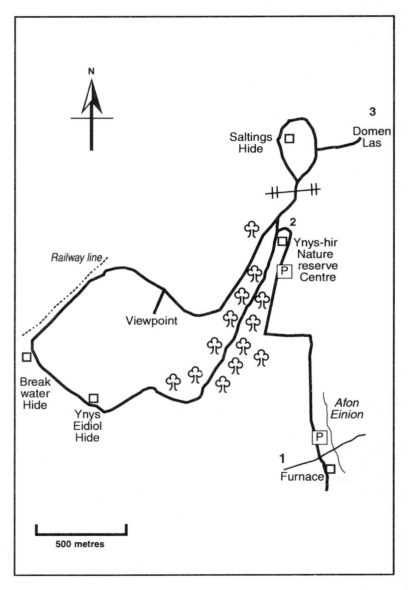

N

3
Domen
Las

Saltings
Hide

2
Ynys-hir
Nature
reserve
Centre

P

Railway line

Viewpoint

*Afon
Einion*

Break
water
Hide

Ynys
Eidiol
Hide

P

1
Furnace

500 metres

2. Ynys-hir RSPB nature reserve comprises a wide range of habitats covering over 1000 acres. The ancient oak woodlands support pied flycatchers, wood warbler, redstart, nuthatch, tree creeper and woodpeckers. In spring there is a carpet of bluebells and wood anemones. Goldcrest may be spotted in the coniferous trees, whilst water rails and warblers breed in the reedbeds. The saltmarshes attract numerous wildfowl, including widgeon, mallard, teal, tufted duck, shoveller and red-breasted merganser. Sundew, bog asphodel and bog rosemary grow in the peat bogs. Birds of prey such as red kite, buzzard and peregrine hunt over the marshes. Many species of butterflies and moths have been found on the reserve, including several uncommon species.

3. Herons nest at Domen Las and the path, hide and motte and bailey castle are not accessible during the breeding season. The motte stands on a rocky ridge overlooking the Dyfi estuary. It was probably built in 1156 by Rhys ap Gruffudd, as a defence against Owain Gwynedd. A few years later it was taken by the Norman lord, Roger de Clare. He rebuilt the castle, but shortly afterwards, Rhys recaptured it.

Walk Directions: (–) denotes Point of Interest

1. At the Dyfi Furnace (1) cross the road to the surfaced track opposite. Pass a car park on the right and walk ahead with Afon Einion on the right. Pass a bungalow on the left and continue along the track to emerge on a lane.

2. Turn left and pass the drive to Ynys-hir Hall. In about 150 metres bear right to follow the signs for the RSPB Ynys-hir nature reserve (2).

3. Facing the reception centre bear right to pass it on your left

and follow a path to a small gate. Turn left on a broad track. In about 100 metres, at a small pond on the left, turn right along a path through woodland to the Ynys-hir hide.

4. Pass the hide on your right and continue along the path to a grassy track. Turn left and cross a track to another path. After crossing a couple of footbridges and passing through reedbeds, you will reach the Covert Du hide.

5. Continue along the path and pass the Ynys Eidiol hide. Cross a footbridge and go through a gate to emerge on a track. Cross to a stile and follow a path to the Breakwater hide.

6. Pass the hide on your left and continue along the path. Cross a stile and walk along with the railway line on your left. Cross a footbridge on your right and walk away from the railway line.

7. On reaching a fork, turn right along the track and cross a stile at a gate. In about 40 metres, leave the main track to bear left. A path on the right leads to the top of a small hill, a fine viewpoint with a bench.

8. Return the same way down the hill and walk ahead to a small gate. Follow a board walk through trees and emerge on a broad track. Turn left and, when there is a gate ahead, bear right on a path to have a fence on your left.

9. When the path enters woodland, bear left and ignore a path on the right. Emerge on a track and turn right. In a few metres, at a junction, bear left on a wide track. Go through a gate and cross a bridge over the railway line. Go through a small gate on the left and in a few paces, at a fork, take the left-hand path.

10. Pass a pool on the left. Go through a small gate on the left and cross a footbridge. Continue along the path and pass the Saltings hide on your right. The path bears right to a stile. The

stile and path on the left leads to Domen Las (closed February – July) (3).

11. Return to the main path. From here you can walk uphill to the Marian Mawr hide. Continue along the path to have a fence on the left. On reaching a path junction, bear left to cross the railway bridge and return along the track to the junction met earlier.

12. Walk ahead and go through a gate. In a few paces, bear left to return to the reception centre. Retrace your steps to the start at Furnace.

Facilities:

Alternative parking, refreshments and toilets at Ynys-hir Nature Reserve.

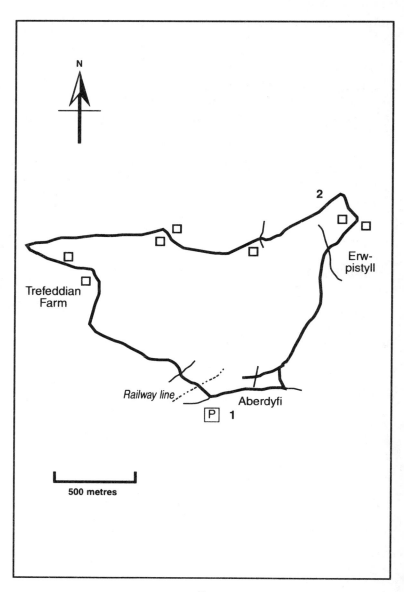

N

2

□   □

□

□   □   □

Erw-
pistyll

Trefeddian
Farm

Railway line

P 1

Aberdyfi

500 metres

Aberdyfi – Erw-pistyll – Trefeddian Farm – Aberdyfi

OS Maps:	1:50 000 Landranger Sheet 135;
	1:25 000 Outdoor Leisure Sheet 23.
Start:	The car park on the sea front in Aberdyfi.
	G.R. 612959.
Access:	Aberdyfi is on the A493, south of Tywyn,
	and 10 miles west of Machynlleth. Trains on
	the Cambrian Coast Line stop here. Bus 29
	from Machynlleth or Tywyn.
Parking:	On the sea front, behind the beach, in
	Aberdyfi.
Grade:	Moderate – paths, tracks and lanes.
Time:	About 2½ hours.

Points of Interest:

1. Aberdyfi, translated into English, means 'the mouth of the Dyfi'. Backed by steep hills to the north, this picturesque resort is situated where the river flows into Cardigan Bay. The name of the village became famous in 1785 when Charles Dibdin composed the song 'The Bells of Aberdyfi'. A comic Welsh character sang the lyrics in the Drury Lane musical 'Liberty Hall'. There are several stories about the bells. One tells of a giant who sat on Cadair Idris and lost his bell, which he had used as a paddle on Afon Dyfi during a storm. Another tells of bells around the necks of lost sheep, as in southern Europe. The best known is that of 'Cantre'r Gwaelod' – see also Walk 2 – the story of the submerging of lands in Cardigan Bay. Although the inundation probably took place at the end of the last Ice Age,

the legend places the event in the 6th century when, it is said, the plain had several churches with beautiful chimes. According to the legend, because of the negligence of the drunken dyke keeper Seithennyn, a great storm breached the walls, and the plain, its towns and inhabitants were lost for ever. Some people say that on windless nights, distant chimes may be heard, rising from the sea bed. The old boundaries of Cantre'r Gwaelod are believed to exist in the form of submerged reefs with Sarn y Bwch to the north (near Tywyn) and Sarn Cynfelin (between Borth and Aberystwyth) to the south.

Little is known of Aberdyfi until 1216, when Llywelyn ap Iorwerth summoned all Welsh rulers to meet him at Aberdyfi. Although popular with herring fishermen, records show Aberdyfi had only three houses in 1569. Less than thirty years later, in 1597, the *Bear of Amsterdam* and its crew of sixty-five Spanish sailors drifted into the Dyfi estuary. Westerly winds prevented her from sailing out, and the Welsh militia did not have the means to take or destroy the ship. It is said that some Spaniards swam ashore and, after hiding in the hills, merged with the local families. When the wind eventually changed, the *Bear of Amsterdam* sailed away but was captured by Drake's navy. In remembrance of this event, there is a café in Aberdyfi called the 'Bear of Amsterdam'. Aberdyfi grew into a busy port and wool, timber and oak bark were exported in the 18th century. Ships were built here and Aberdyfi became the port for the Dyfi valley with the development of local lead, copper and slate mines. A jetty over 100 metres long permitted ships to be unloaded and loaded at all states of the tide. Nowadays, Aberdyfi is well known for its sailing and water sports.

2. On a clear day there are superb views from this lane, and other points on the route, of the Dyfi estuary, Ynys-las, Borth and around the Cardigan Coast to the cliffs of Penfro (Pembrokeshire).

Walk Directions: (–) denotes Point of Interest

1. From the car park on the sea front in Aberdyfi (1), turn right and pass the Tourist Information Centre and gardens on your right. Pass the church on your left and in approximately 100 metres you will reach the Literary Institute. Cross the road to take a path that rises above the road. It zigzags to some steps and eventually emerges on a road.

2. Turn right a few paces then bear left up steps. When the path forks, go right. Bear left, then right, to reach a narrow path that goes uphill through gorse. Cross a stile and walk uphill, bearing slightly left to reach a small slate tip.

3. Bear right and continue ahead on a path. There are fine views of the Dyfi estuary on your right. Pass a waymarked post and bear left along the hill slope to pass above a valley.

4. Go through a small wooden gate. Farther along, go through another gate and walk uphill to a stile. In another 50 metres cross the stream on your right and climb a ladder stile.

5. Walk up the field and in approximately 80 metres bear left through a gap into another field. Bear right and continue uphill. Go through a gap in the bushes into the next field and walk towards the left side of farm buildings. Go through a gate onto a track coming from the farm, Erw-pistyll.

6. Turn left to go through a gate across the track. Walk uphill and, on reaching a lane, turn left (2) downhill and cross a cattle grid. On reaching a junction with another lane, cross directly to a track.

7. Continue ahead to walk behind a house and follow the track to a gate. The track is then enclosed for about 100 metres until it emerges on a surfaced track. Continue ahead with a fence on

your right. The track bears right towards a farm. Go through a gate and walk ahead on the track. Bear left before reaching the farmhouse to pass it on your right.

8. Pass through another gate onto an enclosed track. Do not go through the next gate but walk ahead to have a fence and hedge on your right. At the end of the field, continue beside the fence. After passing through a gate, walk on with the fence on your right.

9. Before reaching the corner, where the fence bears left, turn left to cross the hill. Reach the fence again and follow a track to where it bends right and becomes surfaced. At this point, turn left and descend a grassy track to reach two ruined farm buildings.

10. Pass them on your left and walk around the hillside. Descend to a stile below a farm. Cross a plank over a stream and walk uphill, bearing slightly right, to a gate. Do not go through but bear left and go through another gate into a field. Bear right to pass the farmhouse on your right.

11. Follow a fence on your right to a fenced corner. Turn right to cross a stream and shortly follow a fence on your right. The path rises gently to a footpath signpost. From here there are fine views of the coast and Dyfi estuary.

12. Climb over a couple of stiles and walk downhill with the fence nearby on your right. Pass behind bungalows and cross a ladder stile.

13. Cross directly over a road to the road directly opposite. Follow this road until it ends, then continue on a track. When the track ends at a gate, go ahead on a path.

14. On reaching a junction, turn left to emerge on a road. Bear right and pass under the railway line. At a junction, walk ahead to reach the A493 in Aberdyfi. Turn right to the start of the walk and car park.

Facilities:

Pubs and cafes in Aberdyfi. Public toilets near the start. Visitor Centre.

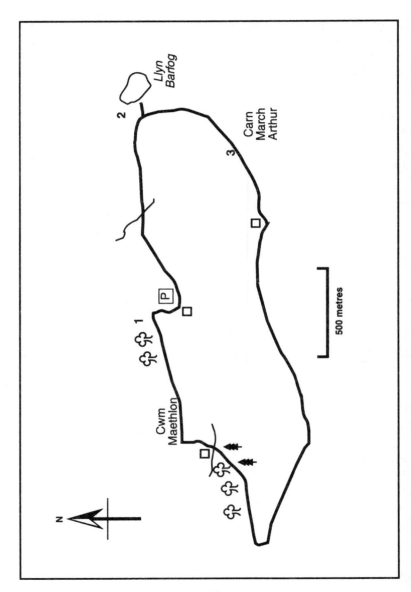

N

Cwm
Maethlon

Llyn
Barfog

2

1

P

3

Carn
March
Arthur

500 metres

Walk 6   *4 miles (6.5 kilometres)*

Cwm Maethlon (Happy Valley) – Llyn Barfog (Bearded Lake) – Panorama Walk – Cwm Maethlon

OS Maps:	1:50 000 Landranger Sheet 135; 1:25 000 Outdoor Leisure Sheet 23.
Start:	Snowdonia National Park car park in Cwm Maethlon. G.R. 641986.
Access:	South of Tywyn, on the A493 to Aberdyfi, take the road signposted Cwm Maethlon (Happy Valley). Or, in the Dyfi Valley, leave the A493 at Cwrt, 4½ miles (7 km) west of Machynlleth.
Parking:	Car park in Cwm Maethlon.
Grade:	Easy/Moderate – paths, tracks, lanes.
Time:	About 2½ hours.

Points of Interest:

1. Cwm Maethlon was known as Cwm Dyffryn before the Victorians started calling it Happy Valley. The road through it is a former turnpike road which connected Machynlleth with Tywyn. The road leaves the Dyfi Valley at Cwrt, near Pennal, and rises to almost 150 metres before starting its long gradual descent through Cwm Maethlon. Just over a kilometre west of the car park, and near the roadside, there is a small chapel. In the graveyard stands a monument to the memory of schoolmaster William Radcliffe who drowned in Afon Dyfi in 1867, at the age of 23.

2. Several legends surround the hillside lake, Llyn Barfog. The name Llyn Barfog (Bearded Lake) may refer to the water lilies

that grow here in summer, or to the legend of the large hairy (bearded) monster that once lived in the lake. It was dragged out of the water by King Arthur or Hu Gadarn (Hu the Mighty) and dragged to Llyn Cau below Cadair Idris. Another legend relates that Llyn Barfog is the dwelling place of Gwyn ap Nudd, the king of the fairies. Long ago, on summer evenings, fairies dressed in green could be seen strolling along the banks of the lake with their greyhounds and white cattle. A local farmer caught one of the fairy cows and she produced a huge quantity of rich milk and gave birth to many fine calves. She became well known in the locality and made the farmer wealthy. However, when the cow became old, he decided that she should be slaughtered. On the appointed day, as the butcher raised his knife, he and the farmer were struck motionless. A lady dressed in green appeared and, when she called the cow's name, the cow and all her progeny crossed the hill and disappeared into the lake. The farmer and butcher were freed from the spell, but neither the cattle nor the fairies were ever seen again.

3. Beside the stone inscribed Craig Carn March Arthur, there is a rock which appears to be indented with the mark of a horse's hoof. It is said that the impression was left by King Arthur's horse when it leapt across the Dyfi estuary to escape enemies. Another legend suggests it was left by the horse after dragging the monster from the lake.

Walk Directions: (–) denotes Point of Interest

1. Leave the car park in Cwm Maethlon (1) by going through the kissing gate in the far right-hand corner. Turn left along the track. Pass farm buildings and cross a stream. Before reaching the house, veer left to cross a ladder stile. The remains of lead mines lie to the right above the farm.

2. Go ahead along the track and cross another stile. In about another 250 metres, shortly before reaching a stream, bear right up the hillside on a path. Cross the stream and follow the path uphill to rejoin the track.

3. The track continues uphill to reach a wall at a ladder stile. Follow the track to another stile. From here a path leads to Llyn Barfog (2).

4. Return to the stile and cross it. The path bears to the right away from the lake. Ignore lesser paths off it. Cross a stile next to a gate and continue beside a fence. Shortly before reaching a stone wall on the left, look on the right for an inscribed stone (3).

5. Continue along the track and cross a stile. From this point there are fine views of the Dyfi estuary. You are now following the Panorama Walk. On reaching two gates near a house, go through the left-hand gate to pass the house on your right.

6. Go through another gate and follow the lane ahead. Soon there are superb views of Cwm Maethlon. Cross a ladder stile beside a gate. The lane is now bordered by fences and passes above a farm and coniferous plantation in Cwm Maethlon.

7. When you reach a point where the lane bears away to the left to go uphill, and the fence on the right veers away from the lane, bear right to follow the fence to a field gate.

8. Go through the gate and follow the clear track ahead as it goes gradually downhill. When you reach a fence at a track junction, bear right to have the fence on your left. Continue downhill.

9. Go through a gate and follow the track through woodland.

Cross a footbridge over Afon Dyffryn–gwyn. Walk ahead to pass a house on the left.

10. Cross a stile near a gate and walk along the drive to a lane. Turn right to follow the lane to the car park and start of the walk.

Facilities:

Full facilities in Tywyn and Aberdyfi. Camp sites at Tywyn.

Pennal – Afon Dyfi – Plas Talgarth – Pennal

OS Maps:	1:50 000 Landranger Sheet 135;
	1:25 000 Outdoor Leisure Sheet 23.
Start:	Pennal Church. G.R. 699003.
Access:	Pennal is on the A493, west of Machynlleth.
	Buses from Machynlleth and Tywyn.
Parking:	Behind the church.
Grade:	Easy – field, riverside and woodland paths, lanes.
Time:	2 hours.

Points of Interest:

1. Pennal church is the only one in Wales to be dedicated to St Peter ad Vincula (St Peter in Chains). St Tannwg and St Eithrias, Celtic missionaries from Brittany, founded a church here in the sixth century, but it was rededicated by the Normans five hundred years later. It has been rebuilt several times since. The circular churchyard indicates early origins. Although the present church is mainly Victorian, it contains some interesting features, including a 'Green Man' in the East Window. Look for the facsimile of the Pennal Letter sent by Owain Glyndŵr in 1406 to the French King Charles VI. In the letter he pledged allegiance to the French Pope in Avignon – at that time Europe had two Popes – provided certain conditions were met. Although normally kept in Paris archives, the original letter was loaned to the National Library at Aberystwyth for six months in AD 2000 as part of an exhibition about Owain Glyndŵr's life. Pennal church was Owain Glyndŵr's Chapel Royal in the year 1406 and he may have signed the letter here.

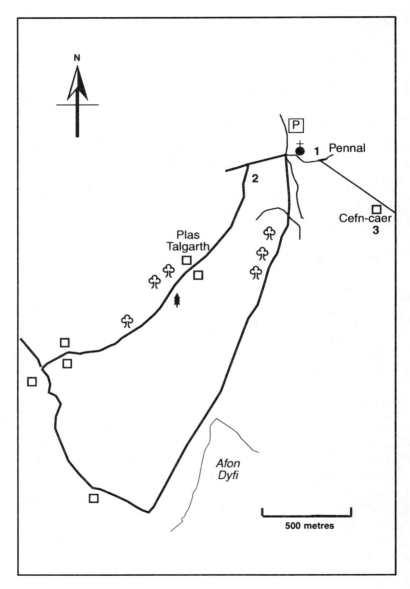

N

P

Pennal **1**

2

Cefn-caer **3**

Plas Talgarth

Afon Dyfi

500 metres

2. The tree covered mound, Tomen Las, is thought to be the site of the medieval court from where Owain Glyndŵr sent the 'Pennal Letter' in 1406.

3. Cefn-caer farm is built in the west corner of the Roman fort. In the field, to the east of the farm, there are signs of foundations in the form of grassy embankments. The fort was sited on Sarn Helen, the Roman road from Caerhun (near Conwy) to *Moridunum* at Caerfyrddin. Roman coins and pottery have been found on the site.

Walk Directions: (–) denotes Point of Interest

1. Face Pennal church (1) and turn left along the A493 to cross the bridge over Afon Pennal. In about 40 metres turn left through a broad gate onto a track.

2. Continue ahead to walk beside the river. Go through a gate across the track. At this point, the track bears right, away from the river. Cross a bridge over a stream and immediately bear right to go through a field gate.

3. Slant left to reach a ditch and continue through the field with the ditch on your right. Pass alongside woodland. At the end of the field go through a small gate and cross a ladder stile.

4. Walk on beside the ditch until you reach a footbridge across it. Cross and turn left. In a few metres, veer slightly right to follow another ditch on your right.

5. On reaching the end of the field, climb to the top of an embankment and turn right to cross a stile. Afon Dyfi is now on your left. Walk along the embankment and ignore a stile below on the right.

6. Look for a footbridge on the right and, after crossing it, walk ahead with a ditch on the left. Before reaching the end of the field, go through a gate on your left. Head towards a farm, and go through a gate to the right of it.

7. Walk up to the lane and follow it uphill. Ignore a track on the left. Continue along the undulating lane. Pass some houses, a track to Penmaenbach, and a bungalow on the left.

8. When the lane descends, cross a stile near a gate on the right. Walk up the field and, at the top of a knoll, go through a gate. Bear slightly left, then right, to pass between buildings.

9. Walk ahead and go through a gate into a field. Continue ahead uphill towards woodland – from here there are fine views of the estuary.

10. On reaching a fence, go through a gate into a strip of woodland. A clear path goes slightly downhill and, in a few metres, has a fence on the right.

11. Follow the path as it levels then goes slightly uphill to a stile. Continue beside the fence and cross a stile into a wood. In a few metres, ignore a path on the left, and walk ahead. On joining a wider path, turn left.

12. The path emerges at the Plas Talgarth holiday complex. Walk ahead to reach the access drive and continue along it to a junction. Turn left to follow a lane between fields.

13. After crossing a stream, you will see the mound, Tomen Las (2) on your right. On reaching the A493, turn right to return to the church in Pennal.

14. If you have time to spare, and would like to see the site of the Roman fort at Pennal, continue along the A493 for about 100

metres, then turn right along a lane. Follow it for about 600 metres, to just beyond the farm of Cefn-caer (3).

Facilities:

Refreshments at the Riverside Hotel. Public toilets behind the church.

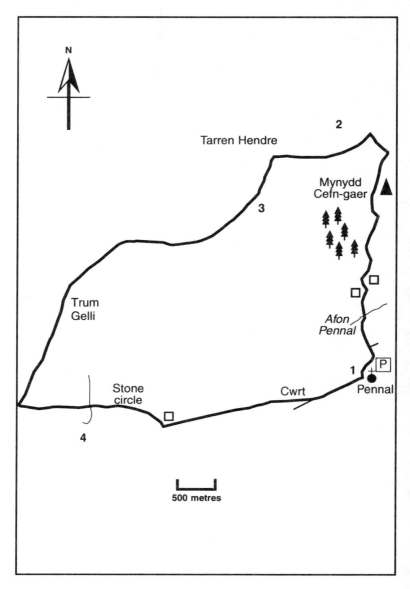

N

2

Tarren Hendre

Mynydd
Cefn-gaer

3

Trum
Gelli

*Afon
Pennal*

P

1

Stone
circle

Cwrt

Pennal

4

500 metres

Pennal – Tarren Hendre – Trum Gelli – Cwrt – Pennal

OS Maps:	1:50 000 Landranger Sheet 135;
	1:25 000 Outdoor Leisure Sheet 23.
Start:	Pennal Church. G.R. 690003.
Access:	Pennal is on the A493 west of Machynlleth.
	Buses from Machynlleth and Tywyn.
Parking:	Behind the church.
Grade:	Strenuous – hill paths, tracks and lanes.
Time:	6-6½ hours.

Points of Interest:

1. Pennal offers much of interest. South-east of the village is the site of a Roman fort known as Cefn Gaer. It was placed to guard approaches by coast and mountain passes to the Dyfi estuary. At one time Roman bricks could be seen in the walls of the church. Inside the building there is a facsimile of the letter Owain Glyndŵr sent to the French King Charles VI in 1406. (To read more about Pennal, see the Points of Interest for Walk 7.)

2. To the north, in the forested valley below, lie the remains of the extensive Bryneglwys quarry. About 300 men were employed at one time and the Tal-y-llyn Railway was built to transport the slate to the main line at Tywyn and then to the port of Aberdyfi. Before the opening of the line in 1866, packhorses carried the slate over the ridge to Pennal. To the north-east of the ridge is Tarren y Gesail, the highest summit of the range (see Walk 12) and, farther north, is Cadair Idris.

3. In clear weather, views from the south-west ridge of Tarren Hendre are exhilarating. To the south, the panorama extends to Pumlumon, the Dyfi foothills and Cardigan Bay. To the north lies the shimmer of Broad Water and the coast curving west below the hills of Llŷn.

4. Llyn Barfog (see Walk 6) and the coast seem tantalizingly close across Cwm Maethlon. When dry, the track offers a delightful walk between outcrops and hillocks. In two kilometres, shortly before a gate across the track, look for a Bronze Age stone circle on a rocky shelf. The circle is fairly small in diameter, with only five low upright stones clearly visible. There is a slab of quartz in the centre.

Walk Directions: (–) denotes Point of Interest

1. From the church in Pennal (1) walk away from the A493. In about 50 metres, at a junction, turn right uphill through Felindre. Pass bungalows on the left and continue uphill along the lane. On reaching a fork, where there is a seat, ignore the right-hand lane.

2. In approximately 600 metres, cross a bridge over Afon Pennal. Ignore the track on the left to Rhosfarch and walk uphill along the lane. Cross a cattle grid and pass a bungalow on the left.

3. Go through a gate across the lane and immediately bear left to cross a ladder stile. Walk uphill and bear right to join a track.

4. Turn left, with a stream below on the right, and follow the track to a gate. Continue along the track, until it emerges in a field. Bear half-right and walk uphill towards the right-hand corner of a forest.

5. Below the forest, follow a track bordered by gorse and go through a gap to cross a stream. Continue along the clear track leading away from the forest. Look back for fine views of the Dyfi estuary.

6. In approximately 400 metres, cross a ladder stile beside a gate. Shortly bear diagonally left uphill to meet a fence rising from the bottom left corner. Continue beside the fence, with a valley below on the left, and the hilltop of Mynydd Cefn-caer on your right.

7. Cross a ladder stile and walk ahead to the next stile, which is beside a gate. Go ahead to a track and turn left. Follow the track around two bends. On reaching sheepfolds, pass them on your left and follow the grass track ahead that rises gradually to the skyline.

8. Turn left along the ridge and pass a ladder stile on your right. Follow the fence uphill (2), cross a stile, and ascend to reach a corner fence near the top of Tarren Hendre. The route turns left here, along the ridge, but to reach the summit cairn (2076 feet/633m), cross the stile ahead, and follow the right-hand fence across the boggy plateau to another junction of fences. Cross the remains of a stile on the right. A small pile of stones marks the summit in a few paces to the left.

9. Return to the ridge path. In a few metres you will pass another small cairn on the opposite side of the fence. In fine weather, this is a superb walk (3). Keep the fence nearby on your right. Follow it for 5 km to the summit cairn on Trum Gelli.

10. Walk on along the ridge to the larger cairn, and cross the fence. In a few metres, the path bears left away from the fence. Follow the clear path downhill and cross a stile. Maintain your direction and in another 500 metres pass through a gap in a

fence to emerge on a track.

11. Turn left along the track (4) and follow it, crossing the occasional stream, for 2 km. After passing a house on the left, emerge on a lane.

12. Turn left along the lane. When it reaches the A493 at Cwrt, go left to return to the start at Pennal.

Facilities:

Refreshments at the Riverside Hotel in Pennal. Public toilets behind the church.

Derwen-las – Cwm Llyfnant – Glaspwll – Derwen-las

OS Maps:	1:50 000 Landranger Sheet 135; 1:25 000 Outdoor Leisure Sheet 23.
Start:	The Black Lion Inn, Derwen-las. G.R. 721991.
Access:	Derwen-las is on the A487, about 3 km west of Machynlleth. Buses from Machynlleth and Aberystwyth.
Parking:	Near the Black Lion Inn.
Grade:	Moderate – field and woodland paths, lanes.
Time:	About 3 hours.

Points of Interest:

1. Over 400 years old, the Black Lion Inn in Derwen-las was a stopping place for cattle drovers and stage coaches. There was a road here in the 17th century and it later became the Machynlleth – Aberystwyth turnpike road. Derwen-las – the name means green oak – was a busy port until the coming of the railway line in the 1860s. Afon Dyfi is tidal up to Dolgelynnen and this enabled ships to sail up the river at high tide. From the quays in Derwen-las – Tafarn Isa, Quay Ellis and Quay Ward – large quantities of timber, oak poles, bark, slate and lead were exported. Imports included rye, wheat, coal, limestone, sugar, tea and soap. Shipbuilding also took place at this small port. When the railway line was built to Aberystwyth in 1863-4, the course of Afon Dyfi was diverted north by the cutting of a new channel. thus isolating the quays. They eventually silted up.

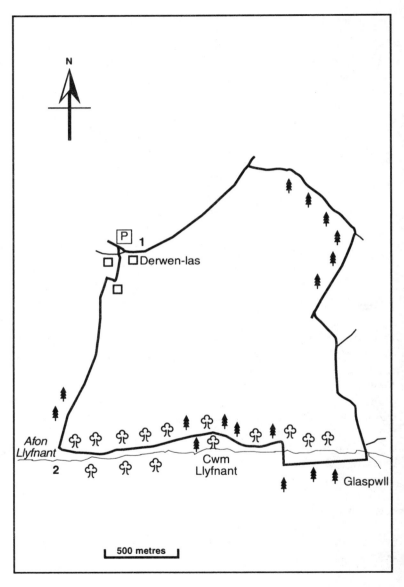

2. The lovely valley known as Cwm Llyfnant is a Site of Special Scientific Interest. It contains remnants of ancient sessile oak and hazel woodlands, with cliffs and boulders covered with ferns and mosses. Dippers may be spotted in the river.

Walk Directions: (−) denotes Point of Interest

1. Face the Black Lion Inn in Derwen-las (1) and turn right to follow a narrow lane uphill. A few metres before reaching a house called Bryn Derwen, take a narrow path leading into the trees.

2. The path zigzags then goes directly uphill to a small gate. Continue uphill beside a fence. On reaching a track near a farm, turn right.

3. Before reaching a left bend on the track, go left uphill on a path to emerge on a lane. Turn left to follow the lane and, when it bends left to a gate, take a grassy path on the right.

4. On reaching a fairly flat area, cross it by keeping to the right. Climb over a stile in the fence ahead. Maintain your direction and walk downhill. In about 200 metres, join a track and shortly go through a gate near the corner fence of a forest.

5. Bear half-left away from the forest and descend to a gate where there is a stream and trees on the left. Go downhill to a grass track and turn left to have a fence on the right.

6. Go through a gate to enter woodland and follow the track through Cwm Llyfnant (2). For a short distance, Afon Llyfnant is close by on the right, but soon the track climbs above it.

7. In about a kilometre, leave the track to follow a clear path on

the right that descends gently between coniferous trees. In about 400 metres the path passes above a field and goes through a gate. Walk ahead and go through another gate to continue on a narrow path. In a few metres, when the path forks, take the left-hand path.

8. The path emerges at a bend on a forest track. Turn right, downhill. A few metres before reaching a gate, turn right on a path. Descend to a footbridge over Afon Llyfnant and walk up to a lane.

9. Turn left and, after passing a house on the left, ignore a track on the right. The lane crosses a stream and the river in the village of Glaspwll. Walk uphill to a junction.

10. Ignore the lane on the right and continue ahead. When the lane divides, take the left-hand fork. At the next lane junction, turn right.

11. In about 600 metres, ignore a lane on the right. Continue to the A487 and turn left to the start of the walk in Derwen-las.

Facilities:

Refreshments at the Black Lion Inn. Full facilities in Machynlleth.

Aberhosan – Esgair Fochnant – Wynford Vaughan Thomas Memorial – Aberhosan

OS Maps:	1:50 000 Landranger Sheet 135; 1:25 000 Explorer Sheet 215.
Start:	Parking area below Aberhosan chapel. G.R. 810974.
Access:	Leave the A489 on the east side of Machynlleth for a road signposted to Dylife. In 4 miles (6.5 km) take a lane on the right signposted Aberhosan. At the chapel take a lane on the right. Parking space is on the left. Postbus from (and to) Machynlleth Monday – Friday.
Parking:	Parking space below the chapel.
Grade:	Moderate – ancient tracks, and lanes, with a long gradual climb to almost 510 metres.
Time:	3-4 hours.

Points of Interest:

1. The isolated village of Aberhosan lies below Foel Fadian, which at 564m is the highest peak in the old county of Montgomeryshire. At one time, the village was well known for its craftsmen, who made and carved bardic chairs for local and National Eisteddfodau.

2. The nature reserve of Glaslyn covers 535 acres of lake, the heather moorland and bog around it, and the ravine below Foel Fadian. Red grouse are able to breed in the reserve – they feed on young heather shoots. Two insectivorous plants, butterwort

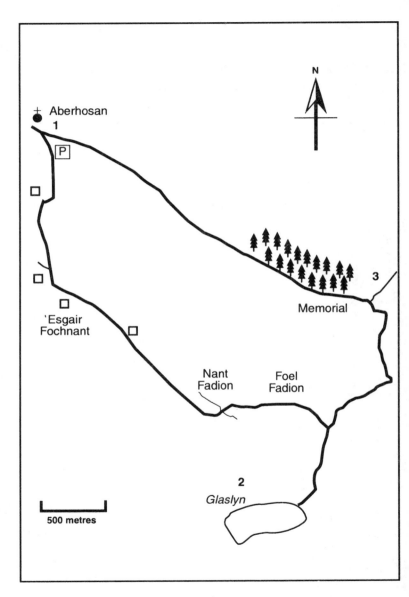

and sundew, grow in the bog. Red kite, buzzard, peregrine and merlin may be seen hunting over the gorge and moorland. A footpath can be followed around the lake but the ravine is dangerous to enter.

3. Wynford Vaughan Thomas considered this spot one of the finest viewpoints in Wales. Born in Swansea in 1908, he became a great writer, broadcaster and traveller. For a time he was Keeper of MSS and Records at the National Library of Wales. He joined the BBC in 1937 and was commentator on royal visits to the Commonwealth. From 1942 he was a BBC war correspondent and received the Croix de Guerre. He made a number of programmes about Wales, and wrote several books before he died in 1987. Unveiled in May 1990, the memorial takes the form of a viewpoint indicator. On a clear day, many distant mountains are visible, including Tarren Hendre, Tarren y Gesail, Cadair Idris, Yr Wyddfa (Snowdon) and Aran Fawddwy.

Walk Directions: (–) denotes Point of Interest

1. From the parking below the chapel in Aberhosan (1), cross the bridge over Nant Blaen-y-cwm and walk uphill through woodland. Bear right with the lane to pass Plas Cefngwyrgrug. The lane bends left to join Owain Glyndŵr's Way and descends to a lane junction.

2. Turn left and follow the lane as it bears right to pass Nantyfyda on the right. Continue on a track that curves to the left to reach Esgair Fochnant.

3. Walk ahead to pass a barn and go through a gate. With a valley below on the left, continue on a track. When the track forks, ignore the left-hand track and walk ahead through a gate.

4. As you walk uphill, Foel Fadian can be seen ahead on the left. Go through another gate and look back to enjoy the views. Cross a stile near a gate and follow the track as it bends left to cross the stream called Nant Fadian.

5. The track bends to the right and crosses bare rock, which can be very slippery when wet. As the track rises there are views to the right over the ravine and to Glaslyn (2). To your left, the summit of Foel Fadian is approximately 100 metres above the track.

6. The track descends to a junction. The route goes left here but, if time permits, a diversion can be made to Glaslyn, by following the track to the right for 800 metres.

7. Continue on the walk by bearing left, or return to this point, and follow the track to a lane. The walk now leaves Owain Glyndŵr's Way. Turn left to pass a millennium milepost on your left.

8. Stay on this lane for about 800 metres. After reaching its highest point, the lane descends. At a bend look for a gate on the left which gives access to the Wynford Vaughan Thomas Memorial (3).

9. Pass the monument on your left and go through a gate. Descend the clear track ahead to have a plantation on your right. When the forest ends, go through the gate ahead and continue along the track to have a fence on your left.

10. Go through two more gates and descend an enclosed track. After passing farm buildings on the left, the track becomes a lane and emerges at houses in Aberhosan. Continue on the lane and bear left just before the chapel to the start at the parking place.

Facilities:

Full facilities in Machynlleth.

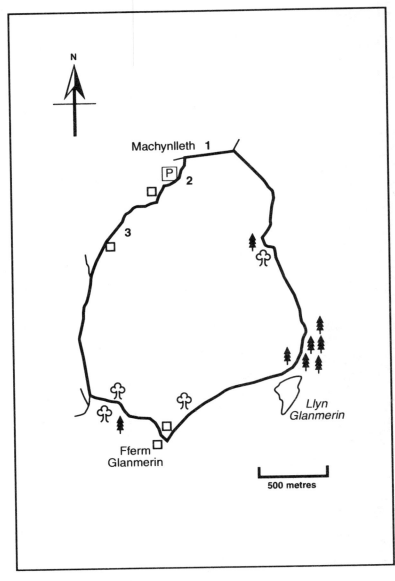

Machynlleth 1

P 2

3

Llyn Glanmerin

Fferm Glanmerin

500 metres

Machynlleth – Roman Steps – Llyn Glanmerin – Machynlleth

OS Maps:	1:50 000 Landranger Sheet 135; 1:25 000 Outdoor Leisure Sheet 23.
Start:	Car park off Maengwyn Street in Machynlleth. G.R. 747007.
Access:	Machynlleth is on the A489, between Dolgellau and Aberystwyth. Trains from Shrewsbury, Aberystwyth and Pwllheli. Buses from Newtown, Dolgellau, Tywyn and Aberystwyth.
Parking:	Town car park off Maengwyn Street.
Grade:	Moderate – field and moorland paths, lanes.
Time:	About 2½ hours.

Points of Interest:

1. Visit Machynlleth on a Wednesday, when Heol Maengwyn is lined with colourful market stalls. In 1291, Edward I granted the Lord of Powys a charter to hold a market at Machynlleth every Wednesday for ever, and two fairs a year. Machynlleth was the town chosen by Owain Glyndŵr to be the capital of Wales. In 1404 it is thought he was crowned here before envoys from Scotland, France and Castile. He held Parliament on the site of Parliament House. North of the clock tower stands Royal House. According to local tradition it is the building where Dafydd Gam was imprisoned after trying to assassinate Owain Glyndŵr, whilst he was being crowned. Henry Tudor is said to have stayed here on his way to Bosworth Field. King Charles may have visited in 1644. An underground passage is said to

run from the house to and under Afon Dyfi, as far as Pennal. The impressive 78 foot (24m) high clock tower was built in 1874 to celebrate the 21st birthday of Viscount Castlereagh, eldest son of the 5th Marquess of Londonderry.

2. In the early part of the 19th century, Y Plas was owned by Sir John Edwards, and it passed to the Londonderry family through marriage. The mansion is mainly 17th century, with 19th century additions. Famous people who have visited Y Plas include Edward VII and Queen Alexandra. It was given to the town in the 1930s and is now home to *Celtica*.

3. The steps were probably cut several centuries later than the Roman period. The Romans probably came this way, however, on their way to the small fort on the hill called Wylfa. It would have been a lookout post for the larger fort at Pennal.

Walk Directions: (–) denotes Point of Interest

1. From the car park in Machynlleth (1), walk out to Heol Maengwyn (the A489) and turn right. Pass the library on your right and, in another 20 metres, bear right through gates to follow a track.

2. The track veers to the right alongside a football ground. Pass the Leisure Centre on your right and shortly turn left to pass Y Plas (2), now *Celtica*, on your right. Pass a children's playground, and then a field on the left. Follow a path to West Lodge.

3. After passing the Lodge, immediately bear left on a path to go through a kissing gate. It leads to the Roman Steps (3). Go up the steps and continue on a path. Go through a kissing gate and cross a track near cottages. Walk uphill on a grassy path to emerge on a lane.

4. Turn left along the lane and ignore a track on the left. Pass a farm and wood on the right and then a track to a house on the left. Descend the lane and, at the point where it swings right to meet another lane, turn left on a track, to have a stream on your right.

5. Go through the gate for Fferm Glanmerin. Follow the track uphill to the farm. Go through a gate and walk ahead to pass a building on the left. Before reaching the farmhouse, turn left on a track. Follow it to a gate and stream.

6. Walk ahead across the field and, in 50 metres, follow a fence on your left. Continue above the fence and pass some woodland. Ignore a field gate on the left and, in another 50 metres, cross a stile beside a gate.

7. Walk ahead uphill between rocky outcrops. Ignore a gate and fence on the right and bear left. The path shortly bears right to reach a stile at a gate. Pass marshy land on the right and go ahead towards the lake called Llyn Glanmerin. Continue beside it.

8. Walk ahead towards a strip of coniferous forest and cross a stile. Follow a path through the trees to a stile on the other side of the plantation. Go ahead on a clear path to have the forest on your right.

9. In about 40 metres, ignore a gate on the right. Walk ahead but bear slightly left on a clear path to have the forest farther distant on your right.

10. Walk ahead over the common. The path veers slightly left towards trees and Machynlleth, which is in view below. Ignore a path on the right going uphill.

11. Bear left to descend towards trees. Continue beside a wall

and trees on the left. Pass above a golf course. The path zigzags –look for posts with yellow arrows – and continue with a fence on the left.

12. After passing a fenced off area, cross a stile and continue ahead to a road. Turn left to a crossroads and turn left along Heol Maengwyn. Pass on your left, a timber framed 17th century house. Continue along the road to the car park and start of the walk.

Facilities:

Public toilets near the start of the walk. Full facilities in Machynlleth. Weekly market on Wednesdays. Owain Glyndŵr Centre. Celtica. Tourist Information Centre.

Walk 12   *6 or 8 miles (9.5 or 13 kilometres)*

Pantperthog – Tarren y Gesail – Nant y Darren – Pantperthog

OS Maps:	1:50 000 Landranger Sheets 124, 135; 1:25 000 Outdoor Leisure Sheet 23.
Start:	Pantperthog. G.R. 749043.
Access:	Pantperthog is on the A487, 2½ miles (4 km) north of Machynlleth, in the direction of Dolgellau. Buses from Machynlleth, Dolgellau and Corris.
Parking:	Small lay-by on the north side of Pantperthog, on the right side of the road if coming from Machynlleth. It is near a telephone kiosk.
Grade:	Moderate – shorter walk. Strenuous – summit of Tarren y Gesail. Forest and moorland paths and tracks.
Time:	4 or 5½ hours.

Points of Interest:

1. A few hundred metres from Pantperthog, on the opposite side of Afon Dulas, is the award winning Centre for Alternative Technology. It is located in the mill area of the disused Llwyngwern quarry, which was in use from the early 1880s to the 1950s. The Centre is a fascinating place to visit, and has many interesting examples of alternative energy sources. These include a water powered cliff railway, solar heating and a wind turbine. There are, also, examples of alternative methods of farming, an educational maze, adventure playground, restaurant and bookshop.

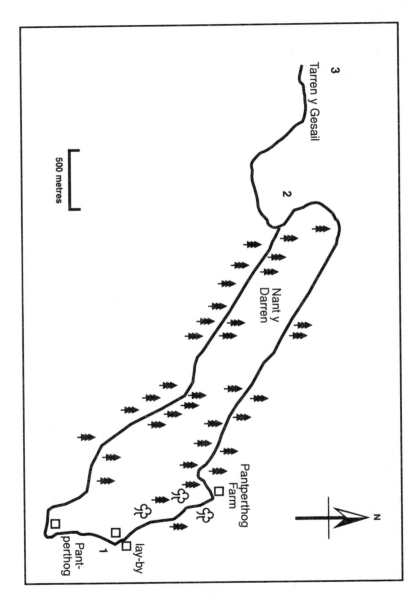

2. Located on an old packhorse route, the Darren quarry has been in use over a long period of time. However, underground workings in the 1850s produced poor quality slate, and difficulties with transport and water power made the site unprofitable. The remains include a small mill.

3. At 2186ft (667m) the grassy summit of Tarren y Gesail is the highest summit of the Tarren range. The peak offers magnificent views, in clear weather, of Cadair Idris north-east, Tarren Hendre to the west and Pumlumon to the south.

Walk Directions: (–) denotes Point of Interest

1. From Pantperthog (1) follow the road towards Machynlleth for 400 metres. Turn right on a track at a footpath signpost and pass a house on the right. Follow the main track when it bears right.

2. In about 100 metres, at a sign for the Esgair Estate, turn left onto a footpath. It becomes wider and emerges on a track. Cross it to go ahead uphill, and continue on a path to reach another track.

3. Turn left and pass a shed on the left. Ignore tracks on the left and right and continue on the main track uphill through the forest. At a fork, go right. There are fine views to your left over Cwm Ysgolion, and ahead towards Tarren y Gesail.

4. On reaching a fork, where the right-hand track goes downhill, take the left-hand track, uphill. When you reach a firmer forest track, continue ahead. In about 100 metres, where the track bends right, follow a lesser track on your left, which goes ahead. This leads, in about 800 metres, to a gate and broken stile on the open hillside of Tarren y Gesail. Walk uphill,

veering slightly right, to reach a wide grassy path. (If you wish to reach the summit of Tarren y Gesail, bear left to pass a disused quarry (2). When you reach corner fences with stiles, do not cross them, but bear right uphill with a fence on your left. On reaching another corner, cross the fence on your left and follow another fence on your right to the trig point (3). Return to the hillside above the forest.)

5. With the forest below on your right, take a path which goes to a small quarry. Cross a stream and, at the quarry, bear right to descend to the forest wall. Follow it on your right to a stile. Cross a stream and emerge at a track junction.

6. Turn right and follow the wide track downhill above Nant y Darren. Ignore a footpath on the left and a descending track on the right. Walk uphill and pass the buildings at Pantperthog Farm on your left.

7. In a few metres, turn right on a clear path. It descends through deciduous and coniferous trees to a path junction. Bear right and, in about 500 metres emerge at a junction of forest tracks.

8. Ignore the immediate track on the left. Bear right for a few metres, then go left to take a lower track, which goes downhill. In about 200 metres, veer left on a grassy track. It emerges on the A487 in Pantperthog. Turn left to the bus stop and parking place.

Facilities:

Refreshments and parking at the Centre for Alternative Technology. Riverside camp site nearby.

Corris – Aberllefenni – Afon Dulas – Corris

OS Maps:	1:50 000 Landranger Sheet 124; 1:25 000 Outdoor Leisure Sheet 23.
Start:	Car park at the Corris Railway Museum. G.R. 754078.
Access:	Corris is off the A487, north of Machynlleth. At the Braich Goch Hotel, turn right into Corris village. Buses from Dolgellau and Machynlleth.
Parking:	Signposted parking at Corris Railway Museum.
Grade:	Easy/Moderate – riverside and forest paths, tracks and lanes.
Time:	About 3 hours.

Points of Interest:

1. Corris lies in the steep valley of Afon Dulas, surrounded by the remains of slate quarrying. The extraction of slate has been the chief factor in the development of the village, although forestry is now the main industry in the area. The planting of the Dyfi forest began in 1926. The Roman road Sarn Helen passed this way and the Romans may have quarried slate in the area. In 1859, a horse-drawn tramway connected the quarries around Corris with the port at Derwen-las on the Dyfi. When the Cambrian Railway opened in 1867, the tramway west of Machynlleth became disused. Steam engines were introduced on the Corris Railway line in 1879 and, for a short while, there was a passenger service. The quarries continued to use the line until 1948, when flood damage to the Dyfi bridge forced its

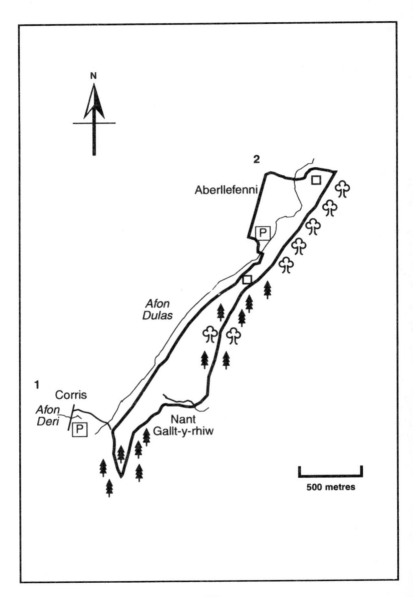

N

2

Aberllefenni

P

Afon
Dulas

1

Corris

Afon
Deri

P

Nant
Gallt-y-rhiw

500 metres

closure. Braich Goch, the largest quarry in Corris, employing about two hundred men, was sited north-east of the village. Since closure in 1971, the area has been landscaped and the main road actually crosses the mill area. Abercorris was another large quarry, situated north of Corris. It was worked until the 1950s, and had both open and underground workings. North-east of Upper Corris are the hillside workings of Abercwmeiddiau, where high walls were built to contain the tipping.

2. Still in use, the Aberllefenni quarry has probably been worked since the 16th century. It produces very high quality slate. The underground workings were connected to the mill by a tramway which was in use until the 1970s. The terminus of the Corris railway was opposite the mill. Remains of the railway can be seen at various places in the valley.

Walk Directions: (–) denotes Point of Interest

1. From the car park walk out to the road and bear right through Corris (1). After crossing Afon Deri, turn right on a lane downhill. Cross Afon Dulas and follow the lane as it bears right. Continue past houses and walk uphill. Pass a track on the right to Fronfelin Hall.

2. In about 100 metres, when the lane starts to descend, turn left on a path that rises into the forest. Ignore a track on the left and continue ahead to reach a wider track.

3. Bear left and, on reaching a fork, go left downhill through an area of felled forest. The track curves around the stream called Nant Gallt-y-rhiw. Ignore a track on the right. Follow the track as it descends, then rises and passes a rough track on the left. In a few paces, take a narrow path on the left which has a

horseshoe waymark.

4. The path is fairly level at first but soon descends through the forest. On reaching a gate, walk ahead with a field on the left and a fence on the right. Cross a ditch and join a track coming from the field. Go downhill and, after going through a gate, ford a stream.

5. On reaching another track, turn right. Pass through a gate and, in a few metres, leave the main track to follow a grassy track. Ahead, in the side of the mountain, is a large hole which was the entrance to underground slate workings. Go through another gate and follow a fairly level grass track.

6. At a ruin, turn left to cross a stile and walk downhill along the right side of the field. At the bottom, bear left to follow a fence above Afon Dulas. Go through a gate on the right into trees, and walk downhill on a wide track. Emerge in a field and walk ahead.

7. Climb over a stile near a gate and cross a footbridge over Afon Dulas. Go through some gates and pass a farm building on the left. Follow the farm drive but, before it reaches the lane, bear left to cross an old bridge.

8. Go up some steps to the lane and turn left. Aberllefenni quarries are on the right (2).

9. Continue along the road and pass the slate mill on the left and houses on the right. Immediately beyond the road sign for Aberllefenni, turn left downhill into a Forestry picnic site and car park.

10. When the track turns left, continue on a gravel path to have Afon Dulas on the left. On reaching a track, turn left to cross a

bridge over the river. Immediately turn right on a track.

11. Cross a bridge over a small stream and bear right to a telegraph pole. Walk along a path to pass the garden of the house on the left. Go through a small gate into a field.

12. Walk beside Afon Dulas. Notice the slate in the river. Continue ahead through the fields, crossing stiles. When the last field narrows, walk ahead on a path through woodland, beside the river.

13. Climb over a stile and continue on a clear path some distance from the river. Cross a stream by stepping stones and a fence type stile. Walk through a field by keeping slightly uphill from the river. Pass a small gate on the left and cross a stream. Maintain your direction to reach a broad gate, and enter woodland.

14. Continue ahead on a clear track. Go uphill to join another track. Bear right to pass above a quarry. Go through a broad gate and continue ahead.

15. Emerge on a lane and turn right to retrace your steps into Corris and the start of the walk.

Facilities:

Alternative parking at the Forestry Picnic Site near Aberllefenni. Public toilets near the start. Railway museum. Corris Railway. Cafe at Corris Craft Centre on the A487. King Arthur's Labyrinth. Youth hostel in Corris.

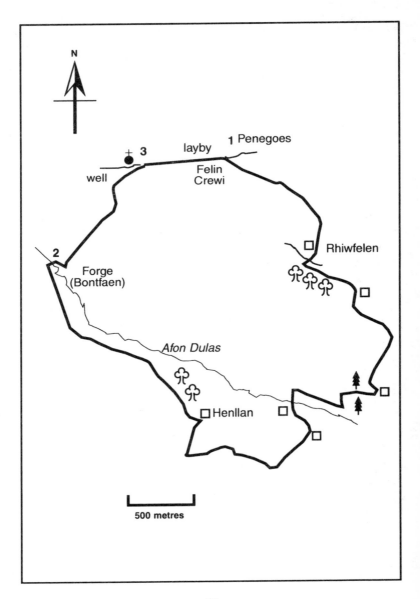

N

1 Penegoes

layby

3 ✛●

well

Felin
Crewi

☐ Rhiwfelen

♣♣♣

☐

2

Forge
(Bontfaen)

Afon Dulas

♣
♣

☐ Henllan   ☐

☐

🌲

🌲 ☐

☐

├─────┤
500 metres

Penegoes – Afon Dulas – Forge – Penegoes

OS Maps:	1:50 000 Landranger Sheet 135; 1:25 000 Explorer Sheet 215.
Start:	Lay-by on the A489 in Penegoes. G.R. 775009.
Access:	Penegoes is on the A489, east of Machynlleth. Buses from Machynlleth and Newtown.
Parking:	Lay-by in Penegoes.
Grade:	Moderate – field paths, tracks and lanes.
Time:	3½ hours.

Points of Interest:

1. The rectory in Penegoes is the birthplace of the landscape artist Richard Wilson (1713-82). Having trained in Italy under Zuccarelli, he was also known for his portraits. He died at Llanferres near Denbigh. Joseph Mallord William Turner visited Penegoes on his tour of Wales in 1798. Another visitor to the rectory, in the early 19th century, was Felicia Dorothea Hemans (who wrote the poem 'Casabianca', which has the well-known line: 'The boy stood on the burning deck'). In the 12th century, the Prince of Powys, Owain Cyfeiliog, may have ruled from a fortress on the hill behind the old mansion, Gallt y Llan. Lately, the village has been known for its working watermill, Felin Crewi. Although the water-wheel is still there, it is no longer a working mill.

2. The Welsh name for Forge is Bontfaen, meaning 'stone bridge', but this refers to an older bridge than the present one

spanning Afon Dulas. In the mid 19th century, the main industry here was weaving. At one time, five fulling mills stood on the banks of the river. Nothing remains of them now.

3. The road through Penegoes is believed to date from the Romans. Dedicated to the 6th century St Cadfarch, the medieval church was rebuilt about one hundred and forty years ago. It has a 15th century font. The name of the village is associated with the Celtic chieftain, Egoes. Penegoes translates as Head of Egoes, and the chief's head is said to be buried under oak trees beyond the church. In a field on the opposite side of the road to the church, and about 100 metres west, is a well that is reputed to have healing powers.

Walk Directions: (–) denotes Point of Interest

1. Follow the road away from Machynlleth, and take the first lane on the right. Pass some houses and walk uphill.

2. Turn right along the farm track to Rhiwfelen and pass the farmhouse on your right. Almost immediately, at a fork in the track, bear right through a field gate.

3. Walk down to the right-hand corner of the field, and go through a small gate. Cross the footbridge over Afon Crewi to emerge on a track. Bear left through woodland. In a few metres, leave the track to follow waymarks on the left. Cross a stile in a fence.

4. Bear right to walk uphill through the trees to another waymarked post. Go left and emerge in a field. Follow the right-hand boundary and, close to a corner, cross the fence where it is protected. Pass the buildings of Pant-ystyllen on your left and walk up to the top left-hand fence. Cross the fence at an arrow.

5. Bear left and pass through a hedge into the next field. Walk ahead to cross a stile and bear right, uphill. Veer towards a hedge on the left. At the end of the hedge, pass a fenced off area on your right. Continue uphill and go through a field gate.

6. Walk ahead and cross a stile near a gate. Turn right to reach a forest track. Bear right a few paces, then turn left on a path. Follow a line of telegraph poles through an area of felled forest. The path may be vague at first, but it soon becomes clearer.

7. On reaching trees, the path veers left. Go through a small gate at Cae-heulan and immediately bear right. Descend on a path to a track at a cattle grid. Turn right and follow the main track. When it bears left, continue along it but, in a few metres, bear right down a steep bank. Bear left on a path through woodland to emerge on a lane.

8. Turn right and, in approximately 350 metres, bear left to cross a bridge over Afon Dulas. Pass Felin y Coed on the right and walk uphill. Bear right with the lane and pass a farmhouse on the left. Ignore a track on the left and walk uphill to a junction.

9. Turn right and follow the access lane to Henllan. In the farmyard, bear left between buildings and pass a large barn on the left. Go through a gate and follow a track to a fork.

10. Go right and, in a few metres, at another fork, go right again. There are fine views across the valley. The track gradually descends the hillside. Go through several gates and pass a barn on the right. After joining another track, walk downhill to emerge on a lane.

11. Turn right and walk downhill through the village of Forge (2). At a junction, turn right to cross a bridge over Afon Dulas. In about 100 metres, turn left to follow a quiet lane to the A489.

It emerges directly opposite Penegoes church (3).

12. Turn right and follow the A489 to the lay-by at the start of the walk.

Facilities:

Full facilities in Machynlleth.

Darowen – Nant Gwydol – Fron Goch – Darowen

OS Maps:	1:50 000 Landranger Sheet 135;
	1:25 000 Explorer Sheet 215.
Start:	Darowen Church. G.R. 829018.
Access:	East of Machynlleth, and 1½ miles beyond Penegoes, leave the A489 on a lane signposted Darowen. Turn left at Abercegir. Darowen may also be reached from Commins Coch on the A470. Postal car from Machynlleth. More frequent buses between Newtown and Machynlleth stop at Commins Coch, 1½ miles (2.4 km) from Darowen.
Parking:	Near the church.
Grade:	Moderate – tracks, lanes and hillside paths. The track at the start of the walk can be very wet and slippery after rain.
Time:	2½-3 hours.

Points of Interest:

1. The Church of St Tudur was founded in the 7th century and it is believed that the saint was buried here. His feast day in October was celebrated by a young man being carried aloft around the parish, whilst others beat him with sticks. In 1864, the 14th century church was replaced by the present building at a cost of just over £667. Inside there are some interesting memorial tablets.

2. Known as Maen Llwyd, the standing stone is over two

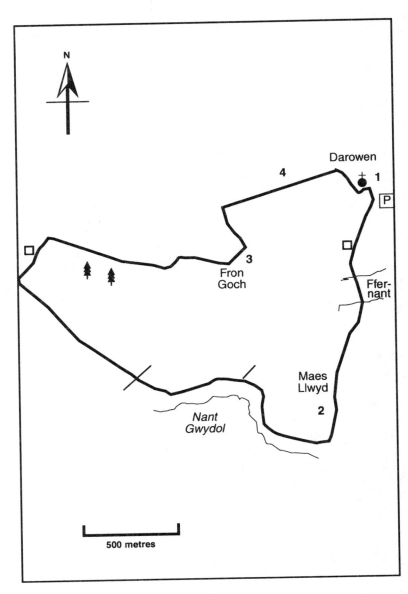

metres high. It is one of three that formed a triangle, and marked a sanctuary or 'noddfa', within which was the village of Darowen. A smaller stone stands north of the village, near Commins Coch. The third stone, which stood to the east, was broken up about one hundred and fifty years ago. In the past, wrongdoers were given the chance to claim their freedom if they could reach the sanctuary before their pursuers. Traces of a church have been found in the area.

3. Remains of the wall and ditch of an Iron Age hillfort can be seen below the summit of Fron Goch. Although only 930 feet (283m) high, the hill offers extensive views of the surrounding countryside. In clear weather, views extend to the peaks of Cadair Idris and Aran Fawddwy. Red kites are sometimes seen flying in the vicinity of Fron Goch.

4. A tree used for hanging once stood on the hill near the present barn. It was chopped down about 1900. The hill is known as Bryn Crogwr, 'Hangman's Hill'.

Walk Directions: (–) denotes Point of Interest

1. With your back to the church gates (1) take the lane almost opposite. In about 30 metres, turn right, downhill.

2. Pass a farm on the right and continue ahead on a track. Descend to the Ffernant valley. Cross two streams, the second by a footbridge, and walk uphill to join a lane. Walk ahead. In about 400 metres, when the lane starts to descend and a track joins from the left, there is a field gate on the right, from which you can see a standing stone (2).

3. Follow the lane downhill. At a junction with a track, bear right to meet another lane.

4. Turn right along the lane. Ignore another lane on the right and continue above Nant Gwydol. In another 300 metres, a few metres before the lane bends right, bear half-right on a path. It climbs through bracken and gorse to emerge on a lane.

5. Cross the lane to continue on a track. It gently climbs the hillside, whilst giving fine views of the nearby hills. In about 700 metres go through a gate and cross a cattle grid. Immediately bear half-right uphill to go through a gate at a corner. Bear left to pass behind a house and go through a gate on the left.

6. Turn right to follow a fence on the right. In about 50 metres it goes steeply downhill to a stile. Walk uphill beside a fence on the right. Pass some coniferous trees and continue near the fence to a gate on your right. Do not go through the gate.

7. Turn left but ignore a track going downhill. Take the higher track that ascends slightly. In about 200 metres, shortly before a gate, join a track coming from the left.

8. Ignore the gate ahead and veer right to follow a wall on the left. When the wall bends to the left, continue uphill to the summit of Fron Goch (3).

9. Walk along the top of the hill and in about 80 metres, when Darowen is in view below, bear left downhill to a stile near a gate. Turn left and follow the wall. Continue beside it, downhill, to reach the corner at the bottom of the field.

10. Cross the stile ahead and veer right to have a fence on your right. Go through a gate. Looking to the left, you will see a barn (4).

11. From the gate, continue ahead with a fence nearby on the right. Cross the stile ahead and maintain your direction through

the field. Pass the end of a fence on the right. Go through a gate opening and turn right.

12. Go through a gate to pass a building on the left. Pass through another gate and follow a track between houses. On reaching a lane, turn left to the church and start of the walk.

Facilities:

Post office/shop at Cemaes Road (Glantwymyn). Full facilities in Machynlleth.

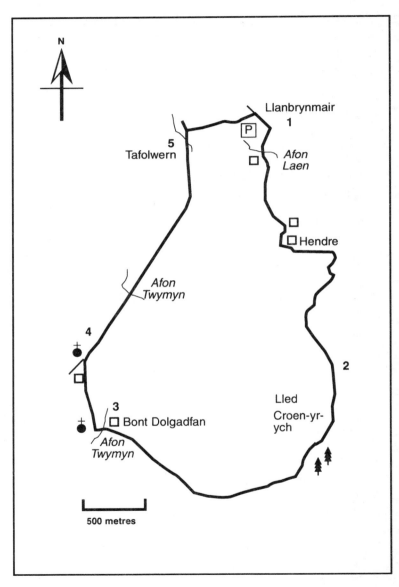

N

Llanbrynmair
1

Tafolwern
5

Afon
Laen

Hendre

Afon
Twymyn

4

Lled
Croen-yr-
ych
2

3 Bont Dolgadfan

Afon
Twymyn

500 metres

Llanbrynmair – Bont Dolgadfan – Tafolwern – Llanbrynmair

OS Maps:	1:50 000 Landranger Sheets 135, 136; 1:25 000 Explorer Sheet 215.
Start:	Car park in Llanbrynmair. G.R. 898028.
Access:	Llanbrynmair is on the A470 south-east of Cemaes Road (Glantwymyn). Buses from Newtown and Machynlleth.
Parking:	In Llanbrynmair, opposite the Wynnstay Arms Hotel.
Grade:	Moderate – moorland and field paths, tracks and lanes.
Time:	About 4 hours.

Points of Interest:

1. The village of Llanbrynmair was originally centred around the parish church, 3 km south of the A470. After 1821, when the turnpike road opened from Newtown to Machynlleth, and the Wynnstay Arms was built as a posting house, people gradually moved down the valley to settle around the hotel. Forty years later the Cambrian Railway reached Llanbrynmair. At that time, the main occupation in the parish was the production of flannel. It was a cottage industry and many people living around Llanbrynmair then, may have been the descendants of Flemish weavers who settled here in the 17th century. When factories in the north of England brought a closure to the cottage woollen industry, many people emigrated to America. It is said that Llanbrynmair provided more emigrants than anywhere else in Wales.

Llanbrynmair has produced some remarkable men. One of the most well-known is Abraham Rees who was born in 1743 and was the son of a pastor of the Independent Church. He also worked in the ministry and in 1778 began editing Chambers Cyclopedia, which came out in parts over nine years. He later wrote Ree's Cyclopedia, which was issued every six months and took forty-five volumes to complete. He received a degree of Doctor of Divinity from Edinburgh and was a member of the Linnean Society. He died in 1825, aged 82. Thirty years later, Samuel Roberts was born in the same chapel house as Abraham Rees, and his father was also a nonconformist pastor. After working on Diosg farm, he became assistant pastor. When his father died he took charge of nine chapels. In 1843, he started writing a magazine called Y Cronicl. He wrote articles condemning slavery, Corn Laws and other causes of human suffering. In 1857, he went to America to join his brother Robert, who had emigrated a year before. However, Samuel Roberts (SR) had severe problems there, and returned home in 1868, where he continued to write.

2. This stone circle on Newydd Fynyddog is known as Lled Croen-yr-ych, meaning the width of the ox's hide. The name derives from a local legend. At one time in the area there were two huge oxen, and for some reason they were separated. One of the pair was tethered on this plateau, and the other on another hilltop. Alone, but in sight of each other, they bellowed in anguish until they died. The circle is over twenty metres in diameter, but the stones are small and inconspicuous from a distance.

3. In the early 19th century a turnpike road passed through Bont Dolgadfan on its way from Llanbrynmair to Machynlleth. At that time, the hamlet had a thriving community engaged in the flannel industry. In 1767 the Calvinistic Methodists built a chapel here.

4. The village of Llanbrynmair was originally centred around the parish church of St Mary, which dates from the 15th century. It is thought that St Cadfan founded a church here in the 7th century – if only for the reason that the name of nearby Dolgadfan translates into meadow of Cadfan. The present church has a wooden tower, and inside there is much of interest, including a 13th century font and an ancient chest. It is surrounded by a circular churchyard, which indicates a Celtic site.

5. The mound to the left is all that remains of Tafolwern motte and bailey castle. During the 12th century it was the seat of Owain Cyfeiliog, a Prince of Powys. After marrying the daughter of his over-lord Owain Gwynedd, he fought with him against Henry II's invasion in 1165. Tafolwern contains the lowest ground in the area and three rivers drain near here, Afon Twymyn, Afon Rhiwsaeson and Afon Laen.

Walk Directions: (–) denotes Point of Interest

1. From the car park in Llanbrynmair (1) turn right along the A470. In a few metres, bear right on the B4518 in the direction of Staylittle.

2. Pass a school and cross a bridge over Afon Laen. In a few paces, before reaching a house, turn left along a track. In about 50 metres, cross a stile on the right. Bear left to another stile that is to the left of a stream.

3. Walk ahead through the field beside the right boundary. Cross a stile and continue with a fence on the right. Climb over a stile on the right and maintain your direction with a hedge on the left. Go through some trees and walk towards a farmhouse.

4. Emerge near farm buildings at Hendre. Bear right and in 30 metres turn left to go through a gate. Bear right to pass through another gate. Walk uphill along a track to cross a stile next to a gate.

5. Bear left along the track. When it bends right, go directly uphill. Bear slightly right and, after passing a waymarked post, slant slightly left to a gate.

6. Go through the gate and bear right beside a fence. On reaching a corner, go uphill to a stile on the right. Emerge on a track and turn left to follow it uphill. In about 600 metres, when the track is less clear, bear left directly uphill to a post with a yellow arrow. Walk ahead to cross a stile.

7. Continue uphill and climb over another stile. Cross the field – a few metres to the left is a low stone circle (2). Go over a stile to have another stone circle on the right.

8. Bear left to cross the next stile. Walk ahead, veering slightly right to walk above a valley. Descend to a small plantation and bear right to have it on your left. Go through a gate to emerge on a track and bear right. In about 60 metres, follow the track around a left bend.

9. Go through two gates and turn right along a lane, downhill. Ignore lanes on the left and right. Cross a bridge over a stream and pass a row of terraced houses at Bont Dolgadfan. Descend to cross a bridge over Afon Twymyn (3).

10. Pass a house on the right and, when the lane bends left, follow a path on the right to a small gate. Pass an old chapel on the left and walk along the right side of the field.

11. Go through a small gate in the right corner and descend to

cross a footbridge. Bear slightly right uphill and walk ahead to cross a track.

12. Walk towards Llan church ahead. Go through a gap in a hedge at a point where a track crosses a stream. Walk uphill through another gap and cross a stile in a corner near a bungalow. Pass a shed and leave the garden through a small gate. Emerge on a lane and turn right. Llan church (4) is on your left.

13. Walk downhill along the B4518 and cross a bridge over Afon Twymyn. In about another kilometre, turn left on a narrow lane. Continue to a lane junction at Tafolwern (5). Turn right to cross a bridge.

14. Bear right on a track. Go through a gate and continue ahead. Bear left to a kissing gate and slant left across the field to a similar gate. Maintain the direction and cross a stile near a broad gate. Continue across fields to a kissing gate at the road. Turn right to the start of the walk at the car park.

Facilities:

Refreshments at the Wynnstay Arms Hotel. Public toilets in the car park.

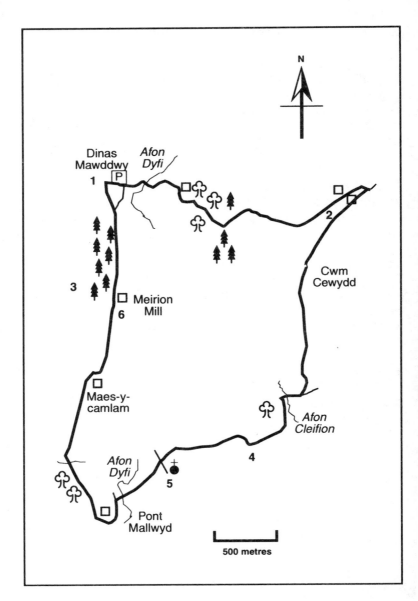

N

Dinas
Mawddwy
P
1

Afon Dyfi

2

Cwm
Cewydd

3

☐ Meirion
Mill
6

☐
Maes-y-
camlam

*Afon
Cleifion*

4

*Afon
Dyfi*

5

☐ Pont
Mallwyd

500 metres

Dinas Mawddwy – Cwm Cewydd – Mallwyd – Dinas Mawddwy

OS Maps:	1:50 000 Landranger Sheet 124; 1:25 000 Outdoor Leisure Sheet 23.
Start:	The Red Lion in Dinas Mawddwy. G.R. 858148.
Access:	Dinas Mawddwy is just off the A470, 10 miles (16 km) east of Dolgellau. Infrequent buses from Machynlleth and Dolgellau.
Parking:	Y Plas – about 100 metres from the Red Lion.
Grade:	Moderate – woodland and hillside paths, tracks and lanes.
Time:	About 4 hours.

Points of Interest:

1. During the 15th and 16th centuries, Dinas Mawddwy was the territory of Gwylliaid Cochion Mawddwy (the Red Bandits of Mawddwy). Such was their notoriety, travellers crossed mountains on their journeys rather than take the road. Houses in the neighbourhood were built with a scythe-blade pointing skywards in the chimneys to deter the bandits from entering from the roofs. They were called Red Bandits because most of them had red hair. They stole cattle and sheep and terrorised everyone. In 1554, Sir John Wynn of Gwydir and Baron Lewis Owen of Dolgellau were authorised to punish them. On Christmas Eve of that year they caught more than eighty of the bandits and all were condemned to death. The mother of two of them begged Baron Owen to spare the life of her youngest son. When he refused, she screamed and tore her blouse to reveal

her breasts and said 'These breasts have given suck to those who shall wash their hands in your blood'. In the following year, Baron Owen was ambushed by the remaining bandits. All those with the baron fled except for his son-in-law, John Llwyd. It is said that the remaining sons of the old woman dipped their hands in his blood. After the baron's death the outlaws were completely exterminated. Dinas Mawddwy became an important centre for lead mining and slate quarrying.

2. Castell is said to have a ghost. A woman who owned this farmhouse had an unfaithful husband. When she died, he forged her will using her dead hand. Later, the ghost of a hand was seen and there were other weird activities including furniture shaking and strange sounds.

3. Over one hundred men worked at the Minllyn slate quarry before it closed about 1916. Tramways took the product to a mill on the valley floor. There are some interesting remains on the site, including the ruined mill, workshops, chimney and a tramway that goes through a tunnel to a pit.

4. It is said that the Red Bandits of Mawddwy were buried near Collfryn, which is just over two kilometres south-east of this point. The lane on your left leads to Gweinion, and continues as a track and a right-of-way. After fording a stream, it goes uphill to a fork. The left-hand track descends towards Colfryn. Before the cottage, at the eastern boundary of the wood on the left, is a large tree covered mound reputed to be the burial place of the bandits. Although not a right-of-way, use of the track is usually permitted to view the burial ground.

5. St Tydecho was a missionary from Brittany and he founded a church on this site in the sixth century. The present building dates from the 14th century and has dormer windows at different levels. Inside are tiered pews and a barrel roof. Above

the porch, dated 1641, are prehistoric animal bones which were dug up nearby about 1850. The Brigands Inn is said to have been the meeting place of the Red Bandits of Mawddwy. George Borrow stayed at the inn: he thought Mallwyd an attractive village.

6. Meirion woollen mill is located in the old station of the former Mawddwy Railway. It ran from Cemaes Road (Glantwymyn) from 1868 to 1951. The coffee shop used to be the station master's house and booking office. Nearby is a 17th century double arched packhorse bridge known as Pont Minllyn.

Walk Directions: (–) denotes Point of Interest

1. From the Y Llew Coch (Red Lion) in Dinas Mawddwy (1) take the minor road signposted Llanymawddwy. Walk downhill and in about 100 metres turn right on a clear track.

2. Cross a footbridge over Afon Dyfi and, with the river on your left, follow a path to a kissing gate. Immediately bear right and pass through a gap which once had a gate onto an enclosed track. After going through a gate, bear right beside a fence. Pass through another gate and emerge on a track.

3. Turn right along the track and pass a house on the left. In about another 100 metres, where the track bears right, leave it to go ahead through a gate. Walk up to a footpath signpost then bear left to follow a fence on your left. Cross a stile into a wood and continue beside the fence. In about 15 metres turn right on a clear path, uphill.

4. At the top of the wood climb over a stile and cross the field diagonally left. Go through trees to cross the field boundary and in about 10 metres cross a stile on the left. Bear right along

an old track. On reaching a corner, veer left on the track to have a wood on your right. As you climb higher there are lovely views across the Dyfi valley to Cwm Cywarch and the Aran mountains.

5. Continue along the track and pass through a number of gates. After a left bend it descends to have views of Cwm Cewydd on the right. Go through another gate and, at the track junction, bear right. Pass farm buildings and walk downhill to emerge on a lane.

6. Turn right past Castell (2) and continue along the lane. In 1.5 kilometres ignore an access lane on the right. Continue to a lane junction. Turn left for a few metres then bear right on another lane that descends to the A458. Turn right and in about 50 metres cross a bridge over Afon Cleifion. Immediately bear left over a stile.

7. Descend to walk along with the river on your left. In about 100 metres, leave the river to bear right uphill through trees to a field. Slant left to a fence. With the fence on your left, walk uphill. After passing through more trees, continue uphill to a corner fence. Bear right and, at the end of the fence, join a track.

8. Turn right along the track and follow it to a gate. From here you can look across the Dyfi valley to the remains of Minllyn quarry (3) above Coed Foeldinas. Emerge on an access lane (4) and bear right, downhill.

9. The lane descends to the A458. (A few metres to the right there is a cafe at the Texaco garage.) Turn left to Brigands Inn and the junction with the A470. About 100 metres to the left stands the interesting 14th century church dedicated to St Tydecho (5). At the road junction, cross to the minor road opposite.

10. Follow the lane to Pont Mallwyd spanning Afon Dyfi. On reaching a lane junction, turn left for about 100 metres. Immediately after passing the garden of a house called Bryn Ffynon on your right, and opposite a track on your left, go through a gate on your right.

11. Walk ahead on a track and follow it when it bears right to another gate. Walk uphill and, at a fork, ignore a track on the right. Continue uphill and at the next fork, bear right to cross a stream at a ford.

12. Climb a ladder stile and, with the Dyfi valley below on your right, walk across the field. Descend slightly to a stile. With a fence on your right, walk ahead. This field is known as Maes-y-camlan, and is one of the many sites attributed to where King Arthur is said to have fought his last battle against Mordred.

13. At the end of the fence, pass through a gate. Immediately bear right to go through more gates and pass farm buildings on the right. Emerge on a lane and turn left.

14. In about 550 metres, after the lane crosses a stream, a path on the right leads to Meirion Mill (6). Continue along the lane to the A470. If you visit the mill, leave by the exit onto the main road. Turn left along the A470 and, after passing a garage, bear right along a road signposted Dinas Mawddwy. It leads to the Red Lion and the start of the walk.

Facilities:

Refreshments at the Red Lion, Mallwyd and Meirion Mill. Public toilets at the start. Camp sites nearby.

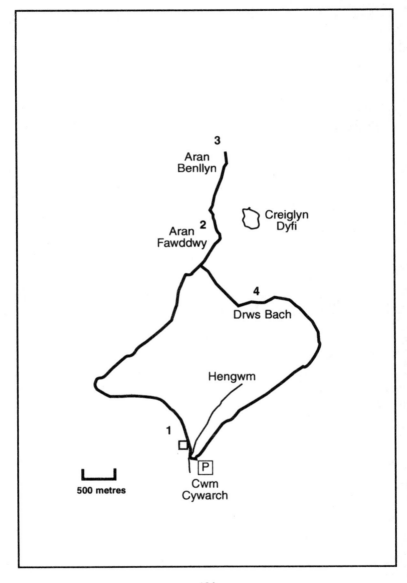

3
Aran
Benllyn

Creiglyn
Dyfi

2
Aran
Fawddwy

4
Drws Bach

Hengwm

1

P

Cwm
Cywarch

500 metres

7½ or 10½ miles
(11.5 or 16.5 kilometres)

Cwm Cywarch – Aran Fawddwy –Aran Benllyn – Drws Bach – Cwm Cywarch

OS Maps:	1:50 000 Landranger Sheet 124;
	1:25 000 Outdoor Leisure Sheet 23.
Start:	Cwm Cywarch. G.R. 853184.
Access:	Leave the A470 at Dinas Mawddwy and take the minor road for Llanymawddwy. Turn left at houses in 1 mile (1.5 km). Parking area in 2½ miles (4 km). Infrequent buses from Machynlleth and Dolgellau to Dinas Mawddwy.
Parking:	At the end of the common in Cwm Cywarch.
Grade:	Strenuous – mountain paths, some steep and rocky. The ascent follows a courtesy path – dogs not allowed. The ridge walk to Aran Benllyn is optional.
Time:	5½ or 7 hours.

Points of Interest:

1. Lead mining has probably taken place in Cwm Cywarch since Roman times. In the 19th century investment in machinery proved unprofitable when less than 350 tons were extracted in seventeen years.

2. Aran Fawddwy at 905 metres (2,971 feet) is the highest peak in southern Snowdonia. On a clear day, magnificent views stretch to Arenig Fawr, Cadair Idris, Yr Wyddfa (Snowdon),

Rhinogydd, Pumlumon and Berwyn. On the summit is a huge pile of stones. It is said that men of Dinas Mawddwy placed them there in the 19th century when told that Cadair Idris was higher. However, their efforts were unnecessary – Cadair Idris is 14 metres lower (44 feet). On the 10th of February, 1945, a Bristol Beaufighter crashed on Aran Fawddwy in low cloud, killing the two members of its crew. Below the high cliffs of the mountain, nestles Creiglyn Dyfi, the source of Afon Dyfi. The stream issuing from the lake is called Llaethnant (milk stream) because of its foamy waters. According to one legend, Saint Decho, who lived in this valley, turned the stream into milk. Another story tells how Maelgwn Gwynedd tried to drive Saint Decho out of the valley by taking away his oxen. Two wild stags came to Decho's aid and pulled the plough for him.

3. At 885 metres, the summit of Aran Benllyn offers superb views towards the Arenig mountains, Hirnant hills and Berwyn. According to legend, the giant Rhitta Fawr was buried on this summit. He collected kings' beards. When he met King Arthur on the slopes of this mountain, he asked for his beard. Arthur refused and in the duel that followed, Rhitta died and was buried on the top of Aran Benllyn. Other versions of this story claim the fight took place on Yr Wyddfa and Rhitta was buried there.

4. The name Drws-bach means little door, the door to Aran Fawddwy. The cairn was built in memory of Michael Robert Aspain, who was killed near this spot by lightning on the 5th of June, 1960. He was on duty with other members of RAF St Athan mountain rescue. They built the cairn. You may like to sign the book in the heavy box. A De Haviland Mosquito of 540 squadron crashed near here in 1944, killing its crew. From this spot there are good views of Creiglyn Dyfi and the Aran ridge.

Walk Directions: (–) denotes Point of Interest

1. From the car park in Cwm Cywarch, continue along the lane. Ignore a footbridge on the right over Afon Cywarch.

2. Before reaching Blaencywarch Farm, turn right through a kissing gate. Walk ahead on a track and shortly bear left. In a few metres, turn right through a gate and continue beside a wall on the left. Continue ahead over stiles beside gates.

3. At the end of the wall, turn left to cross a stile. Walk ahead and shortly bear right to follow the path as it climbs through the valley and passes an old lead mine(1).

4. After crossing a footbridge over a stream, the path becomes rougher and steeper. When wet, the rocks can be very slippery. Follow the yellow arrows.

5. On reaching a fence, follow it on your left, past a ruin, to reach a signpost for Aran Fawddwy. Bear right to pass a pool and follow white topped posts to a stile.

6. After crossing the stile, follow the fence on your right. Cross a couple of stiles and then continue with the fence on your left. Continue beside it to a stile slightly below the south top of Aran Fawddwy.

7. Walk ahead along the ridge to reach the trig point on Aran Fawddwy (2). If it is a clear day, and you have the time and energy, you can extend the walk by following the ridge northwards for 2.5 kilometres to the summit of Aran Benllyn (3). Retrace your steps to Aran Fawddwy.

8. From Aran Fawddwy retrace your steps to the last stile used on the ascent. Instead of crossing it, turn left and descend, with the fence close by on the right. Cross a ladder stile and walk

beside a fence on the left to the memorial cairn on Drws-bach (4).

9. Continue with the fence nearby on the left. At a dip the path leaves it to pass above Hengwm. Cross a ladder stile in the fence ahead.

10. Descend beside the fence for about 600 metres. The path crosses a damp area and, shortly before a rise, it bears right at a waymarked post.

11. Follow the clear path as it descends above the valley called Hengwm. The path crosses a number of streams and becomes fenced after about 2.5 km.

12. When there is a gate ahead, bear right to have a fence nearby on the right. Follow it, ignoring a path on the left, to the footbridge over Afon Cywarch. Turn left to retrace your steps to the start at the car park in Cwm Cywarch.

Facilities:

Portaloo at the car park. Y Llew Coch in Dinas Mawddwy. Coffee shop at Meirion Mill. Camp sites near Dinas Mawddwy.